CROSSCURRENTS *Modern Critiques*

CROSSCURRENTS *Modern Critiques*

Harry T. Moore, *General Editor*

Temira Pachmuss

F. M. Dostoevsky

DUALISM AND SYNTHESIS
OF THE HUMAN SOUL

WITH A PREFACE BY

Harry T. Moore

Carbondale

SOUTHERN ILLINOIS UNIVERSITY PRESS

To Volya and Nina

PREFACE

THE FIRST THING you notice, on reading Dostoevsky, is the way in which he takes you immediately inside the experience he is presenting. Consider The Idiot, whose opening passage is mild enough, describing the approach of a train to fogbound St. Petersburg. But within a few pages, you suddenly know the frail, odd Prince Myshkin, the passionate Rogozhin, and the meddlesome Lebedev: you know them forever. As the story goes on, they develop —particularly Rogozhin and the Prince—they unfold psychologically as few characters in all literature unfold; and after you put the book down, these men and others you meet, as well as the flamboyant Nastasya Filippovna, continue to live in your memory as if they were people you had known, as if the events in which they took part had also involved you. Dostoevsky's ability to create these effects is part of his power.

He was from the first able to cast this magic spell. Despite his sufferings, his imprisonment, and his continual battle against his debts, Dostoevsky never had any trouble getting published, and his books sold readily and widely. His troubles were his own—he was prodigal, and he was a gambler—but from the first he had readers. His books soon appeared in German and French, and eventually in English. Volumes of Dostoevsky, sometimes translated from the French, began to appear in England in the late nineteenth century; Oscar Wilde, reviewing an early version of The Insulted and Injured (as Injury and Insult, by

Dostoieffski), refers to Crime and Punishment, translated
earlier although a later book, and goes so far as to say that,
"since Adam Bede and Le Père Goriot, no more powerful
novel has been written than Insult and Injury."

But Dostoevsky didn't really make an impact in England
until the translations by Constance Garnett, between
1912 and 1920, of twelve volumes of his work. American
enthusiasm for them, which has been intensive, began
some years later. Meanwhile, Dostoevsky's popularity in
Russia, never so great as in the outside world, had waned
during the early years of the Soviet régime, when Dostoevsky seemed one of the properties of the old order of aristo-
crats and bourgeoises. Since then, those who determine
what can and can not be read in Russia have realized that
in Dostoevsky they have a big star, so publication of his
work has been encouraged, with the kind of Marxian
critical reservations that might be expected. A good deal of
valuable new material about him has been unearthed.

Meanwhile, in the America of soap operas and football
crowds and musical comedies, Dostoevsky flourishes. Of
course Americans have certain elements in common with
Russians, some of which are amusingly noted by Rebecca
West in her illuminating preface to Carl Sandburg's
Collected Poems (1926). Dame Rebecca pointed out that
the United States and Russia have great spaces between
the occasional catch-basins of their cities, and that in each
of the countries the majority of the people, not close to
alien borders, are less self-conscious than those in smaller
nations who are continuously and painfully aware of
neighbors. In riding in a taxi in Chicago, Dame Rebecca
was abruptly treated to a long, highly personal monologue
by the driver; she recognized this intense public confes-
sional as the sort of activity that goes on frequently in the
great Russian novels. But there are other, deeper possibilities of similarity to be considered, under the glitter and
noise of American surfaces. One of the nation's most
significant spokesmen, the expatriate Henry James,
summed up American awareness of the depths (which
has produced its "Gothic" from Charles Brockden Brown

and Poe to numerous current writers) when, at the end of
his last great novel, The Golden Bowl, he made Prince
Amerigo tell his wife, "Everything's terrible, cara—in the
heart of man."

The paperback books which are supposedly so emblem-
atic of the superficiality of American reading tastes, but
which have lately become more of an indication of their
depths, have not neglected Dostoevsky: the Spring 1963
issue of Paperbound Books in Print lists thirty-two editions
of his work; and there are of course a number of hardbound
college textbooks and general-reading copies of Dostoevsky's writings available.

The books by Dostoevsky most widely read in American
colleges, and presumably elsewhere in the country, are the
four novels usually considered his greatest: Crime and
Punishment, The Idiot, The Possessed, and The Brothers
Karamazov. The first of these is the most widely studied
and the one with the most obvious features to recommend
it at once to students: it is about a student, and it is a
detective story. But these are only peripheral considerations, as any reader soon discovers: there was never a
student so richly complicated as Raskolnikov, and the
roman-policier aspect of the book is merely incidental to
the dramatized moral problems. For many readers, partly
because Crime and Punishment is the usual introduction
to Dostoevsky, this remains the favorite among his books.
And certainly it is one of the greatest novels ever written.
One can even excuse the extremity of coincidence that
brings Svidrigaylov through the complex vastness of St.
Petersburg to the one room where he can overhear Raskolnikov's confession to Sonya. One can forgive the author
this coincidence because it is part of the necromancy of
the story: Raskolnikov and Svidrigaylov are magically
bound together. And, at the end, each gives himself up to
something beyond himself, Svidrigaylov to death, Raskolnikov to imprisonment. It is part of Dostoevsky's mastery
that he recognizes that it would take another entire book
to show the conversion of Raskolnikov (how different
from "inspirational" novels at the Lloyd C. Douglas level),

a conversion which in Crime and Punishment can be suggested only as a possibility.

The opening passages of The Idiot were mentioned earlier in this preface; it is enough to add here that, although the novel is a crowded and disorganized one, it never loses that first intensity and goes on to an incomparable ending, with its account of Rogozhin forcing Myshkin to stay on the opposite side of the street as they go on their terrible walk through St. Petersburg to that fatal room in Rogozhin's house.

The Possessed, the greatest of all novels about revolutionaries, is also a scattered story, but again it is one which holds its intensity, and the demonic figure of Stavrogin is Dostoevsky's outstanding character up to that time. The Brothers Karamazov provides a gallery of characters of similar magnitude, and it has been pointed out before that, in Dmitry, Ivan, and Alyosha, Dostoevsky was painting variations of a self-portrait: it might be said that Dmitry was what Dostoevsky had been, that Ivan was what he had become, and that Alyosha was what he would have liked to be. This youngest Karamazov, however, was not in Dostoevsky's eyes the purely simple character he sometimes seems: his author makes Alyosha aware of his heritage of the Karamazov strain and sense of guilt.

Like several other late works of Dostoevsky, including The Possessed and A Raw Youth, The Brothers Karamazov derived in part from an earlier grand project of the author's, which he referred to as "The Life of a Great Sinner." There is vague evidence that he planned to write a sequel to Karamazov, perhaps stretching into a trilogy. Ernest J. Simmons, in his excellent volume, Dostoevski: The Making of a Novelist, notes that the story of Alyosha is unfinished, and that he "was obviously destined to undergo the holy pilgrimage of the hero in the plan of 'The Life of a Great Sinner.' In the end, however, Dostoevski's death prevented the fulfilment of the vast design of his great unwritten masterpiece which had nurtured so much of his fiction."

One rumor about the sequel to The Brothers Karamazov is that Alyosha was to become a member of a revolutionary sect and to be put to death for committing a political crime. A more likely rumor is that Dostoevsky intended to send Alyosha out into the world, in obedience to Father Zosima's wish, that he would marry Lisa and leave her for Gruschenka, and then, after a life of sin, would return purified to the monastery as the revered teacher of a group of children. Professor Simmons finds the picture of Alyosha impressive despite its incompleteness. "Had Dostoevski lived to continue it in the sequel, the dream of most of his creative life—to portray a good man on his pilgrimage through sin and suffering to salvation—might have been fulfilled in a characterization of extraordinary grandeur." Another commentator, Julius Meier-Graefe, the rapsodic celebrant of pyramid and temple, takes a different view, saying that an addition to Karamazov would be like supplementing a temple with a second story; to him, the work as it stands is complete. Be that as it may, we have several gigantic novels from Dostoevsky, as well as some supplementary work of great power and interest, such as Notes From the Underground, The House of the Dead, The Gambler, and various other books which take us into that strange world which is one of our world's most absorbing literary experiences, at all times an intensification of everyday reality.

The present book by Temira Pachmuss is an extremely valuable study of Dostoevsky. Miss Pachmuss examines his duality, as it takes different forms which resemble other dualities: the Manichean struggle between light and dark, the conflict between love and hate as reflected in the writings of Henrich von Kleist, the dissociation of personality in the works of E. T. A. Hoffman and others. André Gide, in his book on Dostoevsky, commented on this author's dualism: "I know no writer richer in contradictions and inconsistencies than Dostoevsky." Gide added, "Had he been philosopher instead of novelist, he would certainly have attempted to bring his ideas into line, whereby we would have lost the most precious of them." Miss Pachmuss, aware of Dostoevsky's recognition of the necessity of suffering to attain love, makes a profound exploration of Dostoevsky's duality, and she quotes his early letter to his brother Mikhail (written in 1846, the year of his first novel, Poor People): "They find in me a new and original spirit . . . in that I proceed by analysis and not by synthesis, i.e., I plunge into the depths and, while I dissect the whole into atoms, I bring out the whole." But man's suffering points toward the reconciliation of opposing elements in his nature; and suffering, in Dostoevsky, as Miss Pachmuss defines it, has a far deeper significance than in the customary use of the word.

One of the values of her book, besides its original insights into Dostoevsky's writings, is its citation of a good deal of recent European criticism of this author not usually available to readers in the English-speaking countries. Miss Pachmuss, who has taught Russian at Colorado and Washington (where she obtained her doctorate) and is now at the University of Illinois, of course refers to a good many works available in English, and to a number of authors—Freud, Buber, and Jung, for example—who haven't specialized in Dostoevsky. But she is also able to bring to her argument many recent or current untranslated commentators on this author, including, among Russians, Bakhtin, Dolinin, Glivenko, Lossky, and Mochulsky; among Germans, Bem, Lauth, Nötzel, and Stepun. She has also drawn upon the great collection of Dostoevsky's correspondence in Russian, the last volume of which appeared in 1959.

Throughout, Miss Pachmuss deftly follows her theme, as she investigates book after book, character after character, and idea after idea; and she remains always specific and concrete in her exposition. Her book is a welcome addition to Dostoevsky criticism, and one that Crosscurrents/Modern Critiques is glad to present to readers of modern literature. This fine study of Dostoevsky indeed shows us what Miss Pachmuss means when she writes, "through his revelation, man can be understood more fully."

HARRY T. MOORE

May 11, 1963

CONTENTS

INTRODUCTION

DOSTOEVSKY'S AWARENESS of the human soul's duality and its conquest through integration underlies his philosophy of life and his artistic work. This study is an attempt to trace the development of this theme in his writings. In the religious, philosophical, and ethical ideas, skillfully interwoven in the fabric of his fiction, Dostoevsky expresses a dual concept of the world that appears to have been neglected by critics to a large extent. This neglect, and the relatively limited analysis of the metaphysical background which produced the phenomenon of the double, are the justification for the present examination of the problem of duality in Dostoevsky's works.

Although there is an obvious emphasis on the philosophical and psychological in Dostoevsky's writings, it is well to remember that he is in the first place a novelist. His ideas do not appear as the cold, theoretical products of a philosophical mind; they are formulated and made articulate through the medium of his characters. He does not set forth systems of thought, but recreates life. As an artist and seer, he establishes with his reader not an intellectual, but mainly an intuitive, link, or as D. S. Merczhkovsky says, "It is impossible to read Dostoevsky's books. One must live them; one must suffer with his heroes in order to understand the full depth of his novels." [1] The reader has to make his own discoveries in the vast field of Dostoevsky's philosophical thought. It is left to his subjective comprehension to extract the ideas in Dostoevsky's novels, to trace both the underlying philosophical consistency in his trenchant analysis of spiritual experience and the development of his profound and original thought.

Dostoevsky's vision is steadily directed into the human soul, because he considers man the key to superior metaphysical realities. His awareness of man's spiritual suffering in a God-created world becomes the starting point of his lifelong wanderings in the mysterious depths of the human soul. This awareness establishes a certain similarity between Dostoevsky's outlook and the philosophy of Schopenhauer. Both consider suffering to be such a fundamental factor in human life that they finally identify life with suffering, but their conceptions have important points of difference.

To Schopenhauer, the cause of existence is "the will" as such; to Dostoevsky, it is a duality in the order of the world. He sees two opposite, quite incompatible poles in each phenomenon and each idea. There are life and death, creation and destruction, good and evil, a simultaneous rebellion of man against God in the name of Satan and against Satan in the name of God, and many other such contrasts. Dostoevsky maintains that man, in view of these antitheses in God's creation, tends to regard himself as a transitory creature, as insignificant and meaningless as any other phenomenon on earth. This fills him with despair. Finding such a blow to his self-esteem intolerable, Dostoevsky's hero seeks to find an answer to his dilemma. This leads him to speculate on the purpose of life, and on the nature of life and death. Man's ability to fathom the relationship between life and death is for Dostoevsky the most poignant expression of man's dual nature. His intellect, that quality which distinguishes man from all other animal beings, enables man to grasp this relationship. The intellect stands in contrast to man's animal-personal sphere, yet it dies with his physical death. Since man is exposed to inevitable death, his intellect seems to be not only meaningless and superfluous, but even the immediate cause of his spiritual suffering; for it is his intellect which enables him to recognize the insignificance of his temporal being and discloses to him the duality of his own nature. He can see that man is a creator but also a slave to the causal laws of nature. This revelation is a constant source of torment to man with his pride and with the consciousness of his own divine nature. As a creative spirit, he seeks to achieve spiritual and moral self-perfection; but this process is impeded by his simultaneous striving for self-assertion, or for the gratification of his baser impulses. Unable to reconcile these two diametrically opposed forces, man comes to the tragic conclusion that he—supposedly the greatest of God's creatures because of his intellect, spirit and creative potentialities—is in reality the most imperfect and inconsistent of all created beings. With this discovery, life becomes a state of continual suffering.

Both Schopenhauer and Dostoevsky, having come to this conclusion, seek a way to eliminate suffering. While Schopenhauer sees his possibility in the negation of "the will," a negation which results in the extinction of all life, Dostoevsky has a more optimistic view. He contemplates the disappearance of duality in the world. Without duality there will be no suffering, and man's ideal existence will be attained. However, although Dostoevsky believes in this ideal existence to come, he is still unable to understand the meaning and purpose of man's present earthly state, with its mental anguish. In his efforts to justify man's spiritual pain, he comes to the temporary pessimistic belief, similar to Schopenhauer's, that life is an end in itself, and that it has no further meaning or purpose. But Dostoevsky's passionate idealism does not allow him to make this the permanent conclusion of his philosophical meditations. Tirelessly, he continues his search for the truth; and at the end of his life he believes that he has found it. It is the complete opposite of Schopenhauer's ultimate truth, his "Silberblick der Verneinung." [2] Dostoevsky's belief in the ultimate truth is to be found in his passionate affirmation of suffering and of life with its ordeals.

ii

Certain terms throughout Dostoevsky's work are not used in their generally accepted meaning, but have a broader import. The word "suffering," for instance, in Dostoevsky's novels has a wider meaning than man's usual ordeals. According to his view, suffering is twofold. First, man suffers involuntarily because he is not able to gratify his desires or attain his ideal, if his aspirations are impeded or his potentialities suppressed. He suffers, further, in his rebellion against mental agony, when he violently refuses to accept his fate. In his attempts to free himself from spiritual pain, man often applies means which bring suffering not only to himself but to the people around him. Second, there occurs in Dostoevsky's novels a type of suffering without rebellion. Submitting completely to their destiny, Dostoevsky's passive characters make no attempt to evade their ordeals, but accept them as ordained and justified by God. In consequence they live only for others, specifically for the purpose of loving others. Therefore, the notion of suffering becomes intimately connected with the concept of love.

Dostoevsky's term "love" places more emphasis on the spiritual than the emotional significance of the word. As his Ridiculous Man says, "On our planet we can really love only with suffering, and through suffering." This concept brings Dostoevsky close to Schopenhauer, who maintains that "Alle Liebe ist Mitleid." [3] For the Russian novelist, Christ is the perfect example of this love, since Christ's love is closely related to suffering for the sake of others.

Another of Dostoevsky's terms which is difficult to define is тварное существо. In the opinion of experts, the term "creaturely being" would seem to be the best translation for this expression. In Russian thought the meaning of тварь is twofold. It denotes a "created being," but it also implies a being whose impulses are engendered by his instinct for self-preservation. [4] Man, Dostoevsky says, has been created with these impulses without being consulted by God. Thus, these impulses are natural and tend, Dostoevsky claims, to produce characteristics such as vanity, shame, ambition, hatred, the desire for vengeance, and other manifestations of man's preoccupation with himself to the neglect of others.

iii

In the present work biographical material is used only when it seems to contribute to the general purpose of this study. Citations are newly translated (from the standard Russian editions), except in cases where adequate translations already exist, although here too, when it seemed advisable, changes were made. Due to the lack of some Russian sources, several citations from Dostoevsky's notes are translated from Reinhard Lauth's *Was vermag der Mensch?*, and a smaller number from Karl Nötzel's *Das Leben Dostojewskis*. In all cases other than those acknowledged in the notes, translation from German is by the author of the present volume. Italics are in the original sources.

The writer of this study would like to thank Professor J. Thomas Shaw, Editor of *The Slavic and East European Journal*, for permission to reproduce some material from the *Journal*. Chapter II ("The Technique of Dream-Logic") of the present book appeared, in somewhat different form, as "The Technique of Dream-Logic in the Works of Dostoevskij," New Series, IV, 220–42. Chapter IV ("Symptoms of Spiritual Decay") appeared, in an abridged form, as "The Theme of Vanity in Dostoevskij's Works" in the *Journal*, New Series, VII, 142–59.

The author's most sincere thanks are due to Mr. Boris Christa and Mrs. S. E. Malejew for their advice and criticism; also to Mr. James Dunstan and Miss Dulcie Barraud who have frequently assisted the present writer in various ways.

TEMIRA PACHMUSS

University of Illinois
December 14, 1962

F. M. Dostoevsky

DUALISM AND SYNTHESIS
OF THE HUMAN SOUL

1 DUALITY AS THE SPIRITUAL BACKGROUND

MAN'S QUESTIONS concerning the mystery of his existence in the insensible world arise constantly throughout Dostoevsky's work. He says in his *Diary of a Writer*, "The conviction of life's aimlessness and man's indignation at the inert, inarticulate, all-enveloping universe leads gradually to the inevitable conviction of the absolute absurdity of human existence on earth." [1] Those of Dostoevsky's characters who are unable to reconcile the futility of their existence with the trials imposed upon them by life, turn against God and His creation. "Our planet is not eternal, mankind's duration is just as brief as mine," says the Suicide in "The Verdict," one of Dostoevsky's rebels. His mutiny is prompted by knowledge that behind life hides certain death, and that the earth is slowly cooling, thus contradicting the idea of progress. Similar thoughts are expressed by Ivan Karamazov's devil, who says in answer to one of Ivan's questions, "But our present earth may have been repeated a billion times. It has become extinct, been frozen; cracked, broken to bits; disintegrated into its elements; again water . . . again a comet, again a sun, from the sun it becomes earth, and the same sequence may have been repeated endlessly and insufferably tediously." This endless cycle of decay and regeneration appears meaningless to Ivan Karamazov's devil.

Overwhelmed by the problem of decay, Arkady Dolgoruky in *A Raw Youth* wonders why man should strive for virtue if next day everything is over: "And why should

I be bound to love my neighbor, or your future humanity which I shall never see, and which will in its turn disappear and leave no trace . . . when the earth, too, will be changed into an iceberg; and will fly off into the void with an infinite multitude of similar icebergs; it is the most nonsensical thing one could possibly imagine. . . . Why am I bound to be so noble, especially if it all lasts only for a moment?" If life is only that, Arkady cannot see any reason why he should live in accordance with the law of God and aspire to the harmony and unity of all.

Like Arkady, the Suicide, who is unable to find a key to this apparent lack of meaning in life, refuses to sacrifice himself to anything so pointless. Endowed with intellect, he strives for immortality, if not for his physical being, then at least for his ideas and deeds. His decision to commit suicide is based mainly on his realization that humanity does not exist forever, but lives only a brief moment as compared with eternity. "All right," he argues, "if I were to die, and mankind were to persist forever, then perhaps I might be consoled. . . . But no matter how rationally, happily and piously mankind might organize its life on earth, tomorrow all this world would be made null and void. If all this is necessary, pursuant to some almighty, external and fixed law of nature, believe me, then there is in this idea a most profound disrespect for mankind. To me, it is deeply insulting, and it is all the more unbearable as here there is not one who is guilty."

The Suicide grieves to think that God made him a thinking being, with sufficient intellect only to conceive of the relativity of his existence, his mortality and limitations. Not granted complete knowledge, his mind can proceed only so far as to recognize that nature has set him an intolerable riddle. He asks,

What right had nature to bring me into the world without my consent, with the power of perception which implies suffering. . . . It were much better if I were created like all animals, who live but are not conscious of themselves rationally. . . . I cannot be happy, even with the highest and most *spontaneous* happiness coming from my love for my neighbor and mankind's love for me, for I know that

tomorrow everything will be destroyed. . . . Add to all
this the consideration that this same nature, which allowed
man finally to achieve this happiness, finds it for some
reason necessary to transform all this into nothingness
tomorrow . . . and without even concealing it from me
and from my consciousness, as it does from a cow. . . .
Nature brought me unceremoniously and impertinently
into the world to suffer.

His indignation and anger are aroused by nature's refusal
to answer the vital question, the reason for all existence;
and he feels helpless and unprotected in the face of this
silence. The fear expressed by the Suicide, that he is of no
importance whatever to the "slowly cooling globe," can
deprive man of all joy.

The belief in the earth's ultimate disintegration is so
inconsistent with the idea of immortality that Dostoevsky's hero is perplexed. With his logic he can see under
these conditions only the absurdity of human existence.
Faith, he decides, is quite impossible, a mere abstraction;
it is a waste of time to think seriously about immortality,
against which there is so much material evidence. Fyodor
Pavlovich Karamazov, meditating on this, says to his sons,
"Good Lord! To think what faith, what mental energy
of every kind, man has lavished for nothing on that dream,
and for how many thousand years! Who is it that laughs
at man?" Old Karamazov believes that man's faculties are
too limited to grasp the meaning of a life in which all that
is born is irrevocably exposed to destruction. Man's eternal
cry is "why?" but nature and the Creator maintain their
stony silence. Captain Lebyadkin of *The Possessed* says
to Varvara Petrovna, "You insist on an answer to 'why?'
That little word 'why?' has run through all the universe
from the first day of Creation, and all nature cries every
minute to the Creator 'why?' And for seven thousand
years it has had no answer." A silent creator and nature,
giving no reply to the doubts of man, drive him almost to
despair. They nullify his desire to perform great deeds and
destroy his love for life, so that all he can feel is the utter
inanity of creation.

The Underground Man is engrossed in these considerations of man helplessly exposed to silent nature with its "wall of natural laws." He recognizes his inability to break through this wall and penetrate intellectually the mystery of human existence, but he is not willing to endure this impotence. He believes that thinking man will hardly agree to sit placidly in the place assigned him by nature, even though he knows his efforts to break through the "wall of the laws of nature" are doomed to failure. The Underground Man is aware that his own similar attempt will result in suffering and despair because of his ineffectiveness, or in shame because the human mind cannot penetrate matters transcending the earth. Yet he is not prepared to give up the struggle: "Of course I am not going to break through this wall with my head if I really have not the required strength to do so, yet I am not going to put up with this wall merely because I have run up against it and have not sufficient strength to knock it down."

He considers that a human being who endures unquestioningly the universal law of causality and participates in the ordained and causal physical life, is nothing more than nature's tool. Such a man, with no independent thought, is envisaged as a cow by "the Suicide from boredom," while the Underground Man compares him with a frenzied bull. "A man of that sort goes straight to his goal as a mad bull charges with lowered horns," he reflects, "and nothing but a stone wall will stop him. Such men—that is to say, 'direct' persons and men of action—make no bones about yielding to a wall. . . . For them a wall denotes something restraining, something morally decisive, final and even mystical. . . . Well, I consider such a 'direct' man to be the real, the normal man, as his fond mother, nature, who has borne him kindly upon the earth, intended him to be." Later the Underground Man says, "These people, although under other circumstances they bellow as loudly as bulls, . . . at once become quiet in the face of the impossible. By the impossible I mean the stone wall. What stone wall, do you ask? Well, it is, of course, the wall of the laws of nature." Envying "the real and normal man," who becomes mute before the wall of the impossible, the Underground Man longs for the power to assert himself in complete independence of any outside authority.

Realizing that they are subject to a force outside their own personalities, Dostoevsky's reasoning characters are aware that they must either submit or revolt. The urgent desire to find a solution to the riddle of existence provides a strong motive for the rebellion of Dostoevsky's heroes against God and His creation. In their wish to show their independence and autonomous freedom from God's earth-transcending authority, they may even carry their protest to the point of suicide, as does the eighteen-year-old Ippolit in *The Idiot*. He sees the beauty of earthly life and the joy and exuberance with which nature fills its creatures, but at the same time he also experiences the apparent absurdity of this beauty when death and destruction are inevitable. Knowing that he soon must die, and hating the "blind, silent fate" which, for no apparent reason, has decided to crush him "like a fly," he wants to commit suicide. He envies those who are granted a long life, while he is destined to die young. In the midst of these unhappy thoughts, he recalls Rogozhin, and in his confession writes, "There was such a contrast between us that it could not help being apparent to us both, and especially to me—here was I with my days numbered, and he, a man in the full vigor of life, living in the present, without the slightest thought of a 'final conclusion.' . . . As I rose to depart, I hinted to him that in spite of the contrast and all the difference between us . . . maybe he was not so far from my 'final conclusion.' " Ippolit's "final conclusion" signifies his determination to commit suicide. In a hallucination, he sees Rogozhin entering his room at night, and his "final conclusion" becomes his "final instance of absolute resoluteness." He no longer hesitates to carry out his scheme.

The question could be asked why Rogozhin, of all people, appears in Ippolit's hallucination. They are two quite different people, but Rogozhin is subject to the same silent power of nature as Ippolit. Ippolit is being ruined through his illness; Rogozhin, although "in the full vigor of life," through his passions. Though he possesses all that Ippolit lacks, his happiness is destroyed by the violent emotions with which he has been endowed by nature. From this Ippolit draws the conclusion that not only he, but every living creature, is affected by the powerful force of silent nature. Reflecting on this, he asks himself, "If death is so terrible and the laws of nature so powerful, how can man conquer them? If even He Who conquered nature during His life and to Whom nature was subordinated, was unable to triumph at the end, how much less can man? What hope is there for others, if He had to succumb, He Who in His lifetime could say 'Arise!' and the girl arose, and Who could call to Lazarus to come forth from his grave, and he came forth?" The thought that even Christ, the most elevated and perfect being, should be subject to the meaningless domination of nature, appalls Ippolit. Therefore he is compelled to regard nature as "some huge, implacable and silent monster." Tormented by the image of this monstrous and absurd force, Ippolit longs to have at least one triumph over nature, one action which comes entirely from his own will power.

For Kirillov of *The Possessed*, suicide is the supreme mutiny against nature, which, he believes, is responsible for man's suffering. Considering nature to be the sole creator of all life, Kirillov refuses to be subject to it. He seeks to destroy the existing values; for, in Kirillov's mind, God is only an illusory being, invented by man to replace his subordination to the blind, senseless and despotic force of nature and to free himself from the fear of death. "Man has done nothing," he explains to Pyotr Verkhovensky, "but invent God in order to go on living, and not kill himself; that is the whole universal history until now. I am the first one in the whole history of mankind who would not invent God." By committing suicide, he intends to become a man-god. He wants for once to exercise his own power and display to others an example of man transforming himself into a superman devoid of any fear of almighty nature. Mankind, he insists, must free itself from subjugation to the blind force of causality. Man must develop his own will; he must be proud and free; he must triumph over his fear of death in order to become the master of his own destiny. While he acknowledges the existence of a higher power beyond himself, his actions are necessarily limited; and in his dependence on this power, he is reduced to a low creature trembling before its powerful master.

Other characters in Dostoevsky's works also question man's life on earth. The young intellectual Kraft in *A Raw Youth* is a rebel who prefers suicide to a meaningless existence on earth. The Suicide in "The Verdict" is another who longs to voice his protest against nature, and is resolved to insist on his will by destroying himself rather than "enduring nature's tyranny." Raskolnikov of *Crime and Punishment*, who sees the poverty and suffering of people around him, is at a loss to reconcile the existence of evil with God, the symbol of goodness, mercy, and perfection. In his resolution to kill the old moneylender, he persuades himself to believe that he intends to "do his duty toward humanity" [2] and, by so doing, adjust God's creation. The hero of "The Gentle Maiden" is unable to understand why man is subject to the "gloomy destiny," to the "halting mystery," which makes him its victim and destroys all that is dearest to him.

Some of these characters, like the pawnbroker in "The Gentle Maiden," deprecate the mystery of life and lament over the "gloomy destiny"; some, like Ivan Karamazov, brood over the injustice of God. Although they use dissimilar ways of resisting the mysterious and incomprehensible universal forces, they are all prompted to this defiant attitude toward nature by their awareness of suffering. In Dostoevsky's novels, this suffering appears to be the power which destroys the harmony of the universe. The Suicide, for example, suffers from knowledge of life and death; he is tortured not only by the realization of his own mortality and his personal insignificance on the cosmic level, but also by the consciousness of the eventual decay of all creation. Like an animal, he must care for his bodily needs; therefore he feels himself degraded to the level of a beast. He believes that this dependence on an external force reduces him to the status of a slave rather than a creature made in the divine image.

This feeling is common to all Dostoevsky's rebellious characters. They suffer when their strong impulse for self-preservation compels them to regard those who stand in their way as enemies. Fighting ruthlessly for the gratification of his own interests, Dostoevsky's egocentric hero not only makes others unhappy, but comes to grief himself in this struggle with those of his fellows who are not readily prepared to subordinate their interests to his. As Dostoevsky shows in *Notes from the Underground*, this struggle results in egocentric man's own isolation. The Underground Man, conscious of his baseness, craves self-respect and the respect of others; and in trying to generate this feeling he strives to rise above his fellows and dominate them in order to intensify their feeling of inferiority. He tends to follow the precept of Luzhin in *Crime and Punishment* who says, "Love yourself before everyone else, for everything in the world is based on self-interest."

The question naturally arises, is man to be blamed for seeking self-gratification? The Underground Man overcomes this problem by asking why he has been created with such desires. The guilt, he decides, does not rest with him. The structure of the world itself, as he puts it, is responsible for suffering; for man, without being consulted, has been given the urge of self-preservation at the expense of others.

This theme is further amplified by Shatov of *The Possessed*, who maintains that nations are built up and moved by a force which sways and dominates them: "It is the force of an insatiable desire to go on to the end, though at the same time it denies that end." This end, Dostoevsky believes, is world harmony, or in the formulation of Father Zosima's mysterious visitor, the "Kingdom of Heaven not as a dream, but as a living reality." Ivan

Karamazov describes this "living reality" as a "harmony in which the lion lies down with the lamb, and the victim rises up and embraces the murderer." "All the relations of the world are built on this longing for harmony," Ivan explains to Alyosha, but this harmony cannot be achieved "until everyone becomes really, in actual fact, a brother to all," as the mysterious visitor points out to Zosima.

Universal brotherhood, then, is the ultimate goal of mankind. In order to achieve this goal, the Kingdom of Heaven on earth, mankind must first be unified. But mankind has divided itself into nations and, in this way, resists reaching its goal. The ideals of one nation differ from those of another, as much as does each nation's concept of God. "The object of every national movement, in every pople and at every period of their existence, is only a seeking for a god, who must be their own god, and they must believe in him as the only true god," Shatov says to Stavrogin. IIe finds the discord and disunity among different nations quite logical. He also considers it entirely justifiable that each nation has its own ideals and characteristics. These differences are, for Shatov, the reason why humanity is in a state of continual struggle amongst its component parts. "People have slain each other with the sword," the Grand Inquisitor says to Christ, "they have set up gods and challenged one another: 'Put away your gods and come and worship ours, or we will kill you and your gods!' And so it will be to the end of the world." If nations have no spiritual gods to struggle over, the situation will not be changed. People will replace gods with such idols as money, material wealth, and political doctrines; and they will continue to fight for the sake of these new treasures which have nothing or very little in common with mankind's original notions of good and evil. "When gods disappear from the earth," the Grand Inquisitor points out to Christ, "people will fall down before idols just the same. Thou didst know, Thou couldst not but have known this fundamental secret of human nature." Men have always tried to enforce their own interests with the sword. "It is the force of a persistent assertion of one's own existence, and a denial of death," Shatov believes, which moves nations to struggle one with another. This eternal struggle of mankind does not allow a weakening of the will to live.

According to Shatov, then, the division of mankind into nations is based on a dual force. One side of this force stimulates universal development with love and perfection as its final goal; the other does all it can to destroy this process. Dostoevsky's rebellious characters reveal this duality in the order of the world and in mankind, by the destruction of themselves or others. Through the long process of human development, in Kirillov's words, "from the gorilla to the annihilation of God," nature has produced a man with a high intellectual awareness which enables him to grasp fully the power of nature. But nature allows him to use this knowledge even against itself; he is permitted to impede the process of human development by his destructive will. The suicide destroys himself; the murderer destroys both his victim and his own ideals and potentialities. Man, bearing the image of God, Who urges him to strive for spiritual self-betterment, is imbued at the same time with a destructive will which constantly thwarts this striving.

The duality of the force striving toward and simultaneously denying its end also manifests itself in the Underground Man's "men of action" who, with no independent thought, stimulate through their activities the progress of humanity. According to the Underground Man, a man can remain a "man of action" and participate in this process so long as he feels no inferiority because of his inability to rise above the "wall of the laws of nature." However, once he proceeds to the stage in his intellectual development where he realizes that he is restrained by this wall, he will inevitably lose his desire for action and revolt against these same laws. The Underground Man attempts to prove this point by taking himself as an example.

Dostoevsky expresses the view that the dual principles

in the universe also operate in the human soul. This duality, depicted in his novels, manifests itself in the struggle of man's conflicting urges. His evil has an organic quality—the impulse of self-preservation or the urge of self-assertion—but it also reflects the destructive principle of the dual force which lies behind the universe. Dostoevsky's characters often take delight in evil as such, not simply because they are seeking their advantage, but because of an inexplicable rapture over it. The Underground Man observes that they derive pleasure from destruction; but destruction is evil in Dostoevsky's opinion. This is implied in his draft of *The Possessed*: "Satan is Death and Thirst for Self-destruction." [3] But, despite man's destructive will, man is made in the image of God.

Even Dostoevsky's noble and self-sacrificing heroes reveal this conflict of good and evil, as do all his egocentric characters. Raskolnikov and Svidrigaylov, with their evil impulses, are capable of goodness. Prince Myshkin, with his great love for humanity, his self-sacrifice and self-abnegation, is still capable of evil, and with this his goodness must wrestle. He is loved by Nastasya Filippovna, and he knows that the jealous Rogozhin is capable of killing him because of that love. When Rogozhin actually confesses his feeling of jealousy to the Prince, the latter promises not to visit her. Yet his evil demon awakens and forces him to go to her, knowing that Rogozhin will await him there with murder in his heart. He goes to Nastasya Filippovna with a feeling of a "new and agonizing curiosity," with a "sudden and new idea," which he considers "repulsive and almost impossible." He is ashamed that he could be so suspicious of Rogozhin's intentions; and he is even more ashamed of his own provocative actions. While he tries to convince himself that the purpose of his visit is to see Nastasya Filippovna, rather than to meet Rogozhin, he realizes that the real motive of his visit lies in his "special aim" and "special sudden idea." He feels with despair his "strange and horrid demon upon himself once more," and knows in his mind that he wants Rogozhin to become his murderer. Thus, not only is Rogozhin made to harbor a criminal intention in his heart, but the Prince also is tortured by his own desire to force Rogozhin to suffer from at least a guilty conscience. Both of them reveal the essence of the universal destructive principle. Later the Prince himself admits this to Rogozhin, when he says, "It was our mutual sin."

The humble monk Tikhon in *The Possessed*, a wise, kind and loving man, who has devoted his whole life to helping his fellow men in their spiritual distress, is also aware of the darker tendencies within himself. When Stavrogin takes his confession to Tikhon, the latter tells him that people, after reading the confession, will be startled by its content; they will be horrified and scandalized not by Stavrogin, but by themselves. "They will stand aghast at themselves and will accuse themselves," Tikhon explains to Stavrogin, who is amazed at the monk's low opinion of people. "Ah, do believe me," Tikhon proceeds, "I judge by myself and not by others." Stavrogin is taken aback: "Is this possible? Is there then really something in your soul which now takes delight in my misery?" he asks the monk who humbly replies, "Who knows? Oh, it is possible."

Alyosha Karamazov, who in his loving kindness wishes only the best for others, is also conscious of his evil. He has sympathy for his friend Liza when she tells him of her propensity to do evil things "so that everything might be destroyed." She relates to him her dream of devils: "I have a frightful longing to revile God aloud; and so I begin, and the devils come crowding back to me, delighted, and seize me again, but I cross myself, and they all draw back. It's great fun, it takes one's breath away!" Alyosha admits that he has had the same dream, acknowledging that he, too, knows delight in evil. Dmitry Karamazov expresses the same idea when he maintains that "for the immense majority of people beauty is found in Sodom."

According to the Christian faith, which appears to be the foundation of Dostoevsky's world outlook, the spirit is the divine principle in man. In N. Berdyaev's formulation, "The spiritual . . . becomes a human property, a component part of man; through the Spirit a Divine element is infused into man." [4] The significance which Dostoevsky attaches to the spiritual element in man becomes obvious later in Father Zosima's exhortations. Speaking through him, Dostoevsky calls this element the "spiritual world," which is the "higher part of man's being." To N. L. Ozmidov, Dostoevsky writes, "Your 'I' will not submit itself to the earthly order, but seeks something which transcends the earth, and to which it simultaneously belongs." [5] Through this spirit, which distinguishes man from all other beings, man participates in the "harmony of the universe." The Suicide in "The Verdict" and Ippolit in *The Idiot* interpret this harmony as the aim of all human endeavors and as the final unifying factor of mankind. But man is a dual being, because "he is at once spiritual, supra-natural . . . and also natural." [6] He is the point where two spheres join, the place at which they meet, or as Dmitry Karamazov declares, where "all contradictions exist side by side." Man belongs to two different orders: he is at the same time a spiritual man and a natural man.

This viewpoint has a striking similarity to William Blake's doctrine of man. He held that the tension of human existence results from the fact that man is not only a product of nature, but also a spiritual being; that he is not only an animal, but, in a sense, a god; that he is a citizen of two worlds, in whom the world of eternity and spirit meets the world of time and space. [7]

In his novels, Dostoevsky takes pains to point to this duality and its effect upon human nature. He shows man striving for less mundane values, for spirit and for God, in accordance with the eternal force which leads him to his goal, perfection. He shows also the other side of the dual force which compels man simultaneously to resist the movement toward that goal, and cling more to the earthly aspect of his nature, the main obstacle to spiritual progress. As a creaturely being, Dostoevsky implies in his writings, man must suffer, because suffering originates from man's egocentricity and becomes manifest when he ignores the spiritual part of his nature. His spirit, fettered by his physical body, longs for liberation. In "The Legend of the Grand Inquisitor," Dostoevsky indicates that the tragedy of man lies in his subjection to the impulse for self-preservation, which prevents him from attaining his spiritual goal.

In his writings, Dostoevsky treats implicitly this constraint imposed on man by his bodily nature. As an example, he takes the most natural phenomenon on earth, the very foundation of earthly existence and of the instinct for self-preservation, the impulse for procreation. Man is bound by this instinct, because without it mankind could not exist. "To attain such an exalted goal as personal perfection would be . . . quite meaningless," Dostoevsky writes, "if after attaining it everything should be extinguished and disappear, and if after the attained goal there should be no life for a human being." [8] But

> marriage and unchastity of man are, as it were, the greatest alienation from humanism, the complete separation of the pair from *all others* (there is not much left for all others). The family, or the law of nature is, after all, in the fullest sense a selfish and abnormal state of man. Yet on earth, the family is the most sacred thing to man, for by means of this law of nature man attains his goal through his development, i.e., the sequence of generations. At the same time, however, man must, again according to the law of nature, in the name of his final ideal goal, incessantly deny this very law. This is his duality. [9]

Dostoevsky argues that so long as man is compelled to strive for his final ideal under these conditions, he will yield to the temptation to take his own well-being as his provisional aim. At the same time, however, he will suffer because of his dual nature, for his spirit will strive until the last minute of his life to free itself from the limitations imposed by the physical aspect of his being.

On the one hand, then, man strives for personal betterment and develops his "spiritual world"; and on the other hand, he clings to the opposite aspect of his personality, which is immersed in the natural world. There cannot be an absolute reconciliation between these two contradictory aspects of human nature. The absence of spirit and spiritual life in man is a debasement of the divine image and consequently of man himself. If he renounces the "spiritual world" in his nature and severs himself from God, he is condemned to a divided existence. His life loses its purpose, and he begins to suffer. If, on the other hand, he is resolved to favor his spiritual element, the opposite side will inevitably claim its rights, driven by the powerful instinct of self-preservation.

The basest motives in man exist side by side with the utmost sincerity and purity. Man is endowed with intellect which he can use as freely as he chooses. Therefore he is tempted first to choose the easier way and use his reason not for the benefit of his spirit, but to gratify his creaturely being. The more he indulges in his "flesh and lust," in Raskolnikov's words, the more he departs from his destiny as a spiritual being, a being which strives to remain one with God, with the harmonious unity of the universe. Dostoevsky's novels dramatize this duality in man.[10] They show man in all his hidden perplexities and contradictions and reveal powers of goodness and evil within him such as most men would seldom be ready to acknowledge to themselves. With merciless artistic force, the writer exposes human nature with its deeply rooted conflict between reason and instinct, and the dual struggle between man's spiritual and creaturely being.

THE TECHNIQUE OF
DREAM-LOGIC

RUSSIAN REALISM was formulated as a literary school in the
first half of the nineteenth century, and "in substance it
is a cross between the satirical naturalism of Gogol and an
older sentimental realism revived and represented . . . by
George Sand." [1] While Gogol's naturalism mainly concentrates on the representation of the base sides of humanity in its lower and bizarre aspects, the Russian real-
ists do not caricature man, but depict him as a human
being with good and evil: they take man out of the
slime, but animate him "with the breath of life, and form
a living soul." [2] According to D. S. Mirsky, one of the
principal characteristics of Russian realism is a sympathetic attitude toward human beings, regardless of their
moral or social standing. They are not considered as good
and bad, but only as more or less unhappy and deserving
of sympathy.

Dostoevsky's novels are filled with intense sympathy
for the humiliated, ridiculous, yet still noble human being.
Considering himself a representative of Russian realism,
the writer defines his artistic method in the following way:
"I am a realist in the higher sense of the word, that is, I
explore all the depths of the human soul." [3] This "higher
realism" is at the bottom of his astonishing originality.
In a letter to N. N. Strakhov, he sheds more light on his
notion of realism: "I have my own special view on reality
in art," he writes, "and it is this: what the majority calls
almost fantastic and exceptional, I sometimes hold to be

the inmost essence of reality. Arid observations of everyday trivialities I have long ceased to regard as realism—
it is quite the reverse. In every newspaper you see accounts . . . of the most amazing actual happenings. Our
writers regard them as fantastic, and take no account of
them; and yet they are reality because they are *facts*." [4]

Within this sphere of reality Dostoevsky creates characters that embody the real facts of life in their actions.
His art is symbolical: his "higher realism" sees reality—
or "real reality" in J. C. Powys's terms—through the
veil of earthly phenomena. "The real reality of a person's life is not what they work at, but what goes on in
their minds," [5] writes Powys, defining the power of Dostoevsky as a novelist. Similarly, D. S. Merezhkovsky, considering Dostoevsky's revelation of the irrational and
tragic foundation of the spiritual universe, hails him as a
courageous explorer of the dark labyrinths of the human
soul.[6] E. J. Simmons describes Dostoevsky's artistic skill
in these words: "In realism Dostoevsky created a fourth
dimension which concerned the souls of men and women.
His characters live through their feelings, in the chaos of
passion." [7]

This unique emphasis on the internal world of man
which distinguishes Dostoevsky from preceding Russian
novelists influences his method of characterization. His
choice of subject matter—that is, the underlying inconsistencies of the human soul and its struggle to find its
highest expression—forces him to use a special artistic
technique in dealing with those psychic regions where
mind and intuition are constantly in touch with higher
spiritual realities.

The purpose of this chapter is to examine the technique of dream-logic, one of the artistic devices which Dostoevsky applies in his endeavor to cast light on the
spiritual essence of his heroes, their inner life, and their
subconscious.

In order to present the fundamental conflict, the dis-
parity between objective reality and man's subjective experience, the writer projects himself into the minds of his

characters and identifies himself with their particular world. With his ability to comprehend their inner life, he sees how little their conception of reality corresponds with the objective world. He shows the constant efforts of man to assert his own view of reality and to dismiss the world around him as an illusion and impossibility. Dostoevsky in his works extensively exploits the confusion between these two realms. "We almost always see reality as we *want* to see it," Dostoevsky writes, "as we, in a preconceived way, want to interpret it to ourselves." His opinion is that "we prefer to believe in miracles and impossibilities rather than in truth and reality, which *we do not want to see*." [8]

The writer maintains that this rift between objective reality and man's subjective concept of it is responsible to a large degree for the painful split in the souls of his characters. The portrayal of this disharmony is a fundamental part of Dostoevsky's approach as a novelist, and can be seen in his earliest works. In *Poor Folk*, Makar Devushkin flees from depressing reality into the more pleasant world of his imagination. Although poor and despised by society, he goes to endless pains to give the impression that he possesses sufficient means for a prosperous life. In an attempt to delude his neighbors with regard to his poverty, he even drinks tea, a luxury which he is in no position to afford. While destitute, he makes desperate efforts to convince himself and Varenka that the situation is not so deplorable as it seems; but he himself admits that life appears tolerable to him only when seen through rose-colored glasses. He imagines himself to be madly in love with an actress whom he has never seen. The letter to Varenka in which he relates the story of this love is pathetic in its expression of his desire to escape reality. He goes so far as to buy some scented soap and perfume for his unseen beloved, and hires a carriage to pass by her windows in the manner of a man of the world. As he is too poor to sustain this illusion, he finally has to return to reality, but even then he tries to delude himself by playing the part of a flippant playboy. "Finally I ceased to love her," he writes to Varenka, "I grew tired of her." His struggle against reality appears more poignant when he informs Varenka of his impressions of Gogol's "The Greatcoat." Identifying himself with the hero, Akaky Akakievich, Devushkin is indignant with Gogol for having let Akaky Akakievich suffer as he did. Had he himself been the author of this story, he writes to Varenka, he would have pointed out Akaky Akakievich's virtues, which Gogol failed to do; he would have punished the evil and rewarded the good. In other words, he would have substituted a pleasant dream for painful reality. It is important to note that, although Devushkin's tendency to flee from real life into the world of imagination is quite obvious, the whole representation remains realistic, and Devushkin can always distinguish objective reality from his own world of fancy.

The struggle against reality is also depicted in *The Double*. Here, however, a positive line of demarcation is rarely made between the objective world and the subjective conception of the individual. The irrational element comes forward and plays tricks with reality. The influence of the German Romantic, E. T. A. Hoffmann, whose works Dostoevsky read with enthusiasm at the Military Academy in St. Petersburg, can be observed here. Content, manner, and technique all reveal some similarity to Hoffmann's works, expecially to *Die Elixiere des Teufels*. In Hoffmann's Gothic tale of horror the underlying theme is the incompatibility of everyday reality with human ideals. The phenomenon of schizophrenia is very well presented in the split personality of the monk Medardus. While the spiritual part of his personality is longing for love and purity, he sees his own ego in the abhorrent devil of his double, and succumbs to vice, sensual pleasures, and crime. In *The Double* there are also traces of Gogolian grotesque naturalism. In contrast with Medardus' gruesome and terrible life, the predicament of Gogol's official Kovalyov in "The Nose" represents an extraordinary experience, almost sheer nonsense. He comes upon a part of his ego which was lost to him—

his nose—which is now transformed into another human being with the rank of state councilor. Although both the gruesome element of Hoffmann's artistic form and Gogol's ironic attitude are present in Dostoevsky's *The Double*, they are kept in the background, while the subconscious and irrational sphere of the human soul becomes the center of his interest. The tradition of his romantic predecessors is transformed into a forceful dream-logic with a consistency which, apart from *The Double*, is perhaps to be found only in the works of Franz Kafka.

D. I. Čyževskyj, in his study of the problem of the *Doppelgänger* in Dostoevsky's work, emphasizes Dostoevsky's artistic skill in combining unadorned realism with the means of mystification: "Dostoevskij's style is built on the intermingling of naturalistic and irrational elements. The humdrum and commonplace elements of life are amazingly interlaced with fantastic elements . . . prosaic striving toward reality with ecstatic clairvoyance. . . . Dostoevskij's artistic force lies in the fact that these elements are not simply intermingled, but entwined artistically and so permeated with one another that they constitute an organic unity." [9] R. E. Matlaw, in his illuminating study "Structure and Integration in *Notes from the Underground*," [10] also points out Dostoevsky's great skill in interlacing "naturalistic" representation with elements transcending the bounds of reality: "Dostoevskij's style and his narrative method consist of an interpenetration of 'naturalistic' and metaphysical elements. He introduces real events and philosophical speculations as two facets of the same subject, frequently . . . presenting a naturalistic explanation concomitantly with a mystic one." [11] This artistic technique permits Dostoevsky to leave doubts in the mind of the reader and hero alike as to the line of demarcation between hallucination and reality. Subjective accounts of the hero's delusions alternate with objective descriptions of the physical environment; and the boundary between the realms of hallucination and reality is almost entirely obliterated.

The technique by which Dostoevsky sustains the illusion of the double and the subtlety of his insight into the deranged mind of Golyadkin are impressive indications of the artistic skill of the young author. In spite of the Hoffmannesque element—the juxtaposition of dream life and real life—the central theme of *The Double* seems realistic throughout. As in *Poor Folk,* the underlying idea is the suffering of the human being humiliated in real life and his attempt to create an imaginary world to which he can retreat from his trials and anxieties. However, while Devushkin does not confuse daydreams and reality, Golyadkin tries to make his futile dreams come true. An insoluble conflict between reality and imagination rages in his mind. The whole struggle is woven into an intricate and superb frame of dream-logic, revealing the great artistic talent of Dostoevsky.

The technique of dream-logic plays a very important part in Dostoevsky's artistic method of exploring the irrational depths of the human soul. The "logic" of the dream implies a peculiar causal connection inherent in dreams, which appears essentially alogical in man's waking state. It lacks the characteristics of rational causality and removes the boundary between the world of objective reality and the world of imagination. The events presented by the technique of dream-logic convey the impression of irrationality, and elements from the realm of the subconscious take on the appearance of objective reality. It is through this technique of dream-logic, which obliterates the causal and temporal relationships existing in the world of objective reality, that Dostoevsky depicts the irrational element in man's mind.

The dream technique had already been used in the poems of Tyutchev, very much influenced as he was by the German Romantics in whose conceptual framework dreams played an important part. Interest in the split personality, insight into the dark recesses of the human soul, rejection of surrounding reality and escape into the realm of imagination and of the irrational mind—all these were within the thematic range of the literary works of such German writers as Jean Paul, Novalis, E. T. A.

Hoffmann, to some extent Friedrich Hölderlin, and other writers of the Romantic period. The dream, the hallucination, and the psychological framework already present in German Romanticism on all levels—literary, epistemological, and metaphysical—attain greater depth and wider application in the works of Dostoevsky. In addition, he employs dream-logic as an artistic device more uniformly and consciously.

The technique of dream-logic is extensively used in *The Double*. Golyadkin seeks to belong to the beau monde, but he is aware that a pliant, modest, and meek character would be more in keeping with his frugal means. Therefore he is resolved to overlook all that which is rebellious, evil, and conniving in his own nature. However, as he cannot disavow the existence of all these characteristics, he ascribes them to his nonexistent double. At the office Golyadkin's conduct has always been appropriately humble and pliant. Now, however, he is firmly determined to assert his real ego and change his daydreams, originating in his real character, into reality. This seems to be the main thesis of Dostoevsky in *The Double*. He considers that the world which is commonly perceived by the senses, the rational world, or objective reality, is not real, since people always see reality as they want to see it, as they want to interpret it to themselves. This conviction of the writer finds its artistic expression in Golyadkin's experiences. His colleagues know him as a humble clerk, "who likes to efface himself and slink away in the crowd." This Golyadkin, however, is not the real Golyadkin; he exists only in the minds of his colleagues. Previously he made his conduct conform to their preconceived notions of how a person of his social standing should behave. He has simply adjusted his character to his situation in life, but he is earnestly resolved to be courageous and lay claims to what he considers his human rights. Naturally enough, Golyadkin's ambitions do not conform to the notions of reality held by his superiors. The question which Dostoevsky is posing here seems to be, What is reality? Is it their idea of Golyadkin, or his own conception of himself? The impact of these two conflicting notions of reality is conveyed in masterly fashion. On the one hand, Golyadkin is unable to comprehend the refusal of his superiors to receive him at a dinner to which he imagines he has been invited; and on the other hand, his superiors are unable to understand Golyadkin's impertinence in forcing his way into a party where he is not wanted. Neither, according to Dostoevsky, represents what Powys [12] and others frequently term "real reality." "Real reality" lies in the irrational sphere of Golyadkin's mind. Dostoevsky very graphically brings out the conflict: the struggle of Golyadkin's character, with its urge for self-assertion, against his notion of reality, shaped by the subconscious awareness that he must adjust his nature to the notion of reality held by others.

Dostoevsky likens Golyadkin's irresistible urge for self-assertion to a spring: "Golyadkin dashed forward as though someone had touched a spring in him . . ." "Moved by the same spring which had sent him dashing into the midst of a ball uninvited, he stepped forward." This and similar references stress Golyadkin's irresistible impulse to relinquish his false ego and assert the real one. In this respect the scene on the stairs at the home of councilor Berendeev, Golyadkin's one-time benefactor and patron, appears particularly significant. Golyadkin, convinced of the infallibility of his own notion of reality —which is actually a mere projection of his daydreams— and determined to insist on his appropriate place in society, becomes aggressive. He takes a step forward, while Andrey Filippovich, his immediate superior, jumps back, stupefied at the sight of this new and unknown Golyadkin, who does not correspond in any way to Andrey Filippovich's own idea of his employee. "Golyadkin mounted the stairs more rapidly, and Andrey Filippovich, still more rapidly, darted into the apartment and slammed the door after him," as though symbolically retreating into his own world and eliminating his impertinent subordinate. He is not concerned with the question of whether this resolute conduct manifests the real or the unreal Golyadkin. He is merely anxious to retain his own world, formed in accordance with his perception of reality, and exclude from it anything which does not harmonize.

Golyadkin sees with despair that whichever of his two characters is true, the two conceptions of reality—his own and that of others—are incompatible. This appears to him to be the cause of his failure. After a little thought, he decides to pursue his plan further by cunningly forcing his way to the dinner party through the back entrance. On the landing of the back stairs of Berendeev's apartment, he contemplates the panorama of glittering uniforms and medals, of sparkling wines and aromatic cigars, of the lily-white shoulders and elegant figures of beautiful women. Such a brilliant and sumptuous spectacle has perhaps never appeared to Golyadkin even in his most daring dreams! To stress its splendor and undoubted effect on poor Golyadkin, Dostoevsky pleads his inability to convey all the radiance and magnificence of this dinner, and resorts to the devices of hyperbole and a cliché-ridden language. "Oh, if I were a poet," he laments, "I should certainly have painted all that glorious day with a free brush and brilliant colors! . . . I should describe, then, how, Andrey Filippovich, . . . adorned with the medals that well befit his grey hair, rose from his seat and raised above his head the congratulatory glass of sparkling wine, a wine more like heavenly nectar than plain wine, and brought from a distant kingdom to celebrate such occasions!"

The conception of reality held by Andrey Filippovich and other dignitaries, however, reserves a very minor place indeed for Golyadkin. Dostoevsky conveys this vividly by showing the brilliant party taking place without Golyadkin, although he is present there. "He is also there," Dostoevsky explains, "that is, not at the party, but almost at the party." The following scene, devoid of any glitter or magnificence, constitutes a sharp contrast with the previous brilliance. "Golyadkin is standing huddled in a cold, dark corner which is partly hidden by a huge cupboard and an old screen, in the midst of rubbish, litter, and odds and ends of all sorts . . . watching the course of proceedings as a mere spectator." Driven once more into the background, he feels with profound pain his seclusion from the society which he so much admires. The place where he now stands is being used for storing rubbish. This is symbolic of Golyadkin's idea of his own position in life since he feels himself to be unwanted and entirely worthless. Andrey Filippovich and the others do not notice him standing there any more than they notice him in everyday life, for they belong to a different world. In their world he can participate only as an outsider, as a spectator. Finally he overcomes this feeling of depression and enters the ballroom, possessed by the thought that his rightful place is in this society, but suddenly there comes the awful realization that it is all a mistake. He does not belong there, he feels out of place. As in the scene with Krestyan Ivanovich, all Golyadkin's attempts to appear defiant, self-confident, and complacent fail, and his behavior again betrays him. "On the way he jostled against a councilor and trod on his foot, and accidentally stepped on the dress of a very venerable old lady and tore it a little, pushed against a servant with a tray and then ran against somebody else." He realizes to his despair that, as his presence at the party does not agree with the conception of reality held by others, he will not be able to realize his ideal. With the loss of his own idea of reality, he can no longer find his way in life. He has not been able to assert his true ego, and now he cannot distinguish real from unreal. His world of fantasy and hallucination supplants the world of objective reality, and he has but one desire—to give up all claims to this reality and flee. "There is no doubt whatever that, without blinking an eye, he would have happily sunk into the earth."

Golyadkin's complete derangement is manifest in his confusion at the party, with events and impressions rapidly crowding through his mind. His mental disturbance reaches its peak when he is pushed out onto the cold and dark landing of the stairs. Now, deprived almost entirely of his ability to recognize objective reality, "he feels that he is falling headlong over a precipice." After his disgraceful defeat, his only concern is to escape the reality with which he has failed to cope, and to which others have expected him to adjust his nature. He cannot arrange his whole life according to their requirements and adapt his notion of the world to theirs. From a reality which appears to him painful and unjust, he retreats into an unreal world, into a region of fantasy and the impossible.

The gloomy scene following Golyadkin's headlong flight from reality as others see it reflects the strange and uncanny experiences of his own soul.

> It was an awful November night—wet, foggy, rainy, snowy,
> . . . the wind howled in the deserted streets. It lifted the
> black water of the Fontanka above the mooring rings of the
> river bank, and irritably brushed against the lean lamp-
> posts. The thin, shrill creak of the lamp-posts chimed in
> with the howling of the wind. In the stillness of the night,
> broken only by the distant rumbling of carriages, the howl
> of the wind and the creaking of the lamp-posts, there was
> the dismal sound of the splash and gurgle of water. . . .
> There was not a soul, near or far.

With these details Dostoevsky intensifies Golyadkin's state of despair and perplexity. Now he strives to flee from his real ego, or even to destroy it completely. "He wanted to hide from himself, as though he were trying to run away from himself! Yes! It was really so. One may say more: Golyadkin did not want to escape from himself. He wanted to be obliterated, to cease to exist, to return to dust."

It is in the midst of this agony, while relinquishing the subconscious self with "a feverish tremor running through his veins . . . and possessed by a strange feeling of obscure misery," that Golyadkin's double appears before him. Dostoevsky likens Golyadkin's sensations at this moment to "those of a man standing at the edge of a fearful precipice, while the earth is opening beneath him, shaking, moving, rocking for the last time, falling, drawing him into the abyss." He has longed to free himself from his ambitious and vain ego, which has brought him nothing but suffering, but even after the fulfillment of this longing he has no respite from his panic and agony, for now his double confronts him. Golyadkin's split personality assumes very sharp outlines, and the two men—Golyadkin himself and his double—encounter each other as two separate human beings. This double has all the assertive tendencies of the old Golyadkin, and stands before him stronger than ever, for now Golyadkin has no control over it. In danger of losing the last remnants of his peace and self-confidence, he fights desperately against Golyadkin junior, his double, now his greatest enemy. Losing this battle, he tries again and again to reconcile himself with his double, to become one man. But all his endeavors fail! He refuses to see Golyadkin junior as the incarnation of his own character, preferring to consider him an entirely separate human being, who merely has a striking similarity to himself. He would rather live in a world of "miracles and impossibilities" than admit the truth about himself. Finally his imagination plays him one last trick. The illusion of being loved and respected by society, being reconciled with everybody, even with his tormentor, the double, is granted to him for one brief moment. His daydream is thus converted for him into reality for an instant, and thereafter this same reality crushes him completely.

With great artistic power, Dostoevsky shows in this dream Golyadkin's distress at the clash between his concept of reality and the surrounding world. Here, Golyadkin finds himself in the company of some educated and noble people who like him and esteem his personality. This vision of the triumph and glory produced by his concept of reality is suddenly destroyed by his double. Golyadkin junior, the embodiment of the traits which Golyadkin senior wishes to suppress in himself, "succeeds in proving clearly that Golyadkin senior is not the genuine one at all, but the sham, and that he, Golyadkin junior, is the real one." Thus, in this dream Dostoevsky suggests that the double, the phantom existing in Golyadkin's imagination, represents reality, while Golyadkin himself remains only a vision, a product of his fantasy. It also follows from this dream that Golyadkin's repressed nature is the cause of the subsequent collapse of his conception of reality. This collapse becomes a clear manifestation of the anxiety and neurosis that are preying on his mind. His double—harboring Golyadkin's covert ambitions—urges him to go on living in a manner appropriate to his social standing, and convert his daydreams into reality. Had Golyadkin continued effectively to suppress his subconscious ego, as he had done previously, he would probably have escaped the painful collapse of his illusory world, which would have remained the source of his vitality until the end of his life. Golyadkin's dream, then, revealing his repressed nature, shows at the same time that, in this conflict between the conscious and unconscious of his character, the reality of his conscious ego is overwhelmed and rejected by his "subliminal ego" as a lie.

The final scene in the overcrowded drawing room in *The Double* is particularly significant in revealing Dostoevsky's potent technique of dream-logic, which tends to efface all the causal and temporal relationships of the world of objective reality:

Our hero went into another room; he met with the same attention everywhere; he was vaguely conscious of the whole crowd closely following him, noting every step he took, talking in undertones among themselves of something very interesting, shaking their heads, arguing and discussing in whispers. . . . Suddenly Golyadkin's name was called from the other room; the shout was at once taken up by the whole crowd. All was noise and excitement, all rushed to the door of the first room, almost carrying our hero with them . . . there was a general stir —something they had long been waiting for happened. 'He is coming, he is coming!' passed from one to another in the crowd. 'Who is it that is coming?' floated through Golyadkin's mind, and he shuddered at a strong sensation.

The whole scene makes the impression of a dream, with a dream's peculiar logical connection, throwing light on the psychic symptoms of Golyadkin's irrational ego. The use of dream-logic, which enables Dostoevsky to sustain his unfortunate hero's vision of his double, shows that objective reality and Golyadkin's subjective world of reality ultimately become transformed into two irreconcilable entities: Golyadkin's actuality and its opposite, the actuality of the rest of the world. The irrational reality, superseding the rational, finally becomes for Golyadkin his sole world.

The contrast between the exact fixation of time and Golyadkin's lapses into timelessness is an astute device of the technique of dream-logic. It is a difficult task for the reader to determine the length of time between Golyadkin's first entry into the apartment of Berendeev and his final appearance there in a state of complete mental derangement. On the other hand, Dostoevsky gives the exact time that Golyadkin enters his own apartment and emphasizes his haste to leave it again by eight o'clock. These contrasts intensify the dream-like atmosphere in which the objective world loses its reality through the elimination of the notions of time and space. The dream, in its turn, introduces dream-logic, which focuses the author's attention on the innermost recesses of Golyadkin's dual nature.

The Double remains Dostoevsky's only work in which this form of artistic expression is consistently maintained. In none of his later works does dream-logic occupy such a predominant place; and nowhere does he transform the reality of his central character into a phantom to such an extent as to allow this phantom to dominate the whole situation. Now and then Dostoevsky returns to this artistic form, but—with the possible exception of "The Landlady," where, as in *The Double*, the major conflict lies between the world of reality and the world of imagination into which Ordynov escapes—there is little difficulty in distinguishing reality from hallucination in his later works.

The criticism of Belinsky and other contemporaries, who disliked *The Double*, may be the reason for Dostoevsky's subsequent cautious and limited employment of dream-logic. This defeat must have been particularly painful to him because he expected much from *The Double*.[13] He now began to seek another form of expression; but fragments of the technique so consistently developed in *The Double* are found also in his later works, for example in *Crime and Punishment*. Here Dostoevsky sometimes blurs the border between objective reality and Raskolnikov's conception of reality, making dream and reality merge; and once more he voices his conviction that there is a tendency in man to see the objective reality as he wants to see it. Raskolnikov, prior to his crime, sees his prospective murder as a heroic deed, almost "a duty toward humanity"; he sees himself as an "extraordinary man," almost another Napoleon. Yet, after his crime is committed, he begins to see things in a different perspective, as his previous understanding of reality slowly gives way to reality itself. Now he can no longer believe in the heroic motives of his murder. He realizes that he has murdered solely to satisfy his ambition and vanity. This truth is revealed to him through the unexpected encounter with the artisan who calls him a murderer. This mysterious man with "a morose, stern and discontented look" suddenly appears before Raskolnikov, filling him with horror as he reveals the cruel truth that Raskolnikov has so much feared. As if in a dream, his heart knows more than his mind. Gogol's Danilo in "The Terrible Vengeance" expresses the same idea in his speech to Katerina: "You do not know the tenth part of all that which is already known to your soul." Petrified with fear, Raskolnikov cannot efface from his memory this apparition with its smile of "cold hatred and triumph," an apparition which personifies his own guilty conscience. This dream-like revelation of reality is continued in his dream of another, fruitless attempt to kill the old woman. He is led to her by the same mysterious man, as if he were intent on pointing out once more to Raskolnikov that he is only a murderer, far removed from his idol Napoleon.

Dostoevsky does not distinguish clearly the line of demarcation separating Raskolnikov's waking state from the dream which follows. He does not even mention that Raskolnikov fell asleep; he merely says, "He became oblivious; it seemed strange to him that he did not remember how he had got into the street." Yet the impression of the dream is conveyed by a few illogical observations cunningly woven into the realistic background. The imagery used is no longer concrete. Raskolnikov's remark about the moon shining through the window is an example. "This silence springs from the moon," he reflects, "it must be asking a riddle." A similar effect is also produced by the remark, "the more silent the moon was, the more violently Raskolnikov's heart beat." When Svidrigaylov suddenly emerges before him at the end of the dream, Raskolnikov is not sure whether he is still dreaming and whether Svidrigaylov represents a real man or another apparition. He has never seen him before, yet he is aware of some incomprehensible likeness between them.

Philip Rahv, in a recent study entitled "Dostoevsky in *Crime and Punishment*," expresses his view that "there is no innate relationship between the two, no affinity of the mystical order as is posited in so many Dostoevsky studies." [14] In all fairness to this commentator, it should be noted that even Svidrigaylov himself, realizing his inner kinship with Raskolnikov, points it out to him, "Well, didn't I tell you that we had something in common? . . . When I came in a few minutes ago and saw you lying with closed eyes, pretending to be asleep, I said to myself at once, 'This is the very same man!' "

In what respect is Raskolnikov "the very same man"? What is the basis of their mutual understanding? Unlike Golyadkin's double, Svidrigaylov has an objective existence. He is a real human being. And yet he is as much a part of Raskolnikov's subsconscious being as Golyadkin is of his. When he looks upon this facet of his real ego, as incarnated in the personality of Svidrigay-lov, Raskolnikov loathes its repulsive nature, but the invisible thread connecting them is sustained throughout the novel. As if in a dream, he comes across Svidrigaylov when he has not the slightest idea where to look for him. Both of them acknowledge the fact of their inner likeness, their inner connection with each other. Throughout his life, Svidrigaylov's chief aim has been self-indulgence, and in striving to gratify all his desires he falls prey to perversions, which ultimately result in his guilty conscience. Like Raskolnikov, he is no longer able to experience a passionate feeling of love or hatred. He sees his life as meaningless, devoid of any deep and genuine emotion. His appearance before Raskolnikov emphasizes the warning previously sounded by the artisan: that Raskolnikov will end up in the same spiritual impasse if he persists in living only for ambition and vanity. It is a final reminder that these are untenable as a basis for a life-giving morality. Here, again, Dostoevsky shows that Raskolnikov's conception of reality has misled him; it has compelled him to regard his ambitious striving for power and domination as heroic courage. Engrossed in his own idea, he has overlooked reality, overlooked his own real self, his subconscious, in the same way that Golyadkin did.

Within the realistic framework of *Crime and Punishment*, Dostoevsky introduces elements of a technique which both contrasts and simultaneously merges dream-logic with reality. The approach in *The Idiot* is essentially different. Here Dostoevsky paints a great canvas of realistic detail but covers it as though with a veil of dreams. The dream-logic shows itself mainly in the interrelationship of the characters. They know the thoughts and feelings of others sufficiently to have a foreknowledge of their actions. For example, everybody present knows why Ippolit reads his confession and speaks his innermost thoughts, although he has not previously discussed these subjects. They all know beforehand that he will not shoot himself even though he is determined to commit suicide. The answer is frequently given before the question has been asked. When Ferdyshchenko, requested at Nastasya Filippovna's birthday party to relate the worst of his evil actions, tells the guests of the theft he has committed, he anticipates Prince Myshkin's observation which subsequently comes true. The characters are seldom surprised by any unexpected event, for they appear to have a presentiment of all these happenings. Even though Aglaya's love for Prince Myshkin has never been mentioned, all her relatives and friends are aware of it. Nastasya Filippovna, while living far away from St. Petersburg, has a knowledge of Aglaya's love for the Prince, but no indication is given as to how she could have obtained this information. All the characters move and speak as if in a dream in which people appear and events happen with little logical coherence. Sometimes the heroes manifest the power of foretelling the future. Nastasya Filippovna, Rogozhin and Prince Myshkin, all have a foreboding that Nastasya Filippovna will be murdered by Rogozhin long before it actually happens. Similarly, Prince Myshkin knows that Rogozhin contemplates murdering him.

However, in this novel, too, we find scenes in which, as in *The Double* and *Crime and Punishment*, dream merges with reality. Such is, for example, Rogozhin's appearance before Ippolit, a scene which is strongly reminiscent of the first dream-like meeting of Raskolnikov and Svidrigaylov. It is in a hallucination that Ippolit sees Rogozhin entering his room at night, but Dostoevsky describes their meeting so realistically that not only Ippolit but even the reader himself begins to have doubts as to whether it is only an apparition. Rogozhin, wearing a tail-coat and a white tie, enters the room, quietly closes the door, goes to the little table under the icon-lamp in the corner, and silently sits down, leaning with his elbow on the table. He looks at Ippolit with a mocking smile in his eyes, then stands up, quietly, "almost on tip-toe," goes to the door, opens it, and leaves the room, again carefully closing the door behind himself. Ippolit is able to establish only the next morning that Rogozhin in the flesh could not have come in, as all the doors were locked at night.

A consistent development of Dostoevsky's earlier conviction that man is helplessly exposed to the pitfalls of the objective world, while he tries desperately to flee into his own world of imagination, is also evident in this novel. The theme of contrast between actual and subjective realities is further developed in the person of General Ivolgin. He mitigates the painful impact of objective reality by lapsing into the world of his morbid imagination. Here Dostoevsky once more raises the question What is reality? He says here that there is no clear definition of reality: "Almost every reality, even if it has its own immutable laws, nearly always is incredible as well as improbable. Occasionally, moreover, the more real, the more improbable it is."

In contrast to Shakespeare and other great playwrights who build their tragic effect to a large extent on man's inability to cope with the situations in which he is placed, Dostoevsky makes the destiny of his characters dependent on man's subsconscious "impulse of destruction." This feature of human nature is artistically delineated in *The Idiot*, especially in the dream-like encounter of Prince Myshkin and Rogozhin, who is armed with a knife. While he is intuitively aware of what could happen, the Prince feels himself irresistibly drawn toward the waiting Rogozhin. The dream-like impression is carried further by the Prince's fear of Rogozhin's glowing eyes, which repel and yet attract him at the same time. Instead of fleeing from Rogozhin, Prince Myshkin visits him in order to convince him that he is neither his rival in love nor an enemy, but his loyal and loving friend. But even while he seeks to divert him from thoughts of murder, Prince Myshkin knows that his efforts will prove vain. Rogozhin, although acknowledging his rival's friendship and brotherly love, and understanding his feeling of pity for Nastasya Filippovna, is still unable to master his urge to murder the Prince. After wrestling with his desire to avoid meeting Rogozhin, the Prince finally succumbs to his still stronger yearning to see his friend as a murderer. His inner struggle to evade Rogozhin's knife and yet to provoke in him his "urge for destruction," is conveyed by means of Dostoevsky's dream-logic. With a distinct premonition of the imminent disaster, the Prince yields to the temptation of seeing reality as he wishes to see it. His exclamation, "Parfyon, I won't believe it!" as Rogozhin raises his knife, may signify Myshkin's desperate will to replace unbearable reality with a more pleasant lie. In spite of the dream-logic in this scene, Dostoevsky does not forget to account for the Prince's clairvoyance realistically by introducing an epileptic attack during which he allegedly experiences moments of supreme knowledge.

Possibly encouraged by the success of *The Idiot*, Dostoevsky is less concerned with the likelihood of events in *The Eternal Husband*, a work which Alfred Bem designates as an "unfolded dream." [15] In Bem's instructive interpretation, the real happenings which take place before the eyes of the reader are merely the dramatized visions of a morbid imagination. The dream did not merge with reality, as Velchaninov thought, but turned into visions, which he mistook for reality. According to Bem, the whole story is "a tragedy of conscience," "an idea of crime and punishment," the core of the tragedy being not an external punishment but an inner consciousness of and expiation for sin.

The artistic representation of *The Eternal Husband* resembles more closely that of *The Double*, but there is a considerable change in the dream-logic. The baser passions of Golyadkin and Raskolnikov are embodied in their alter egos, Golyadkin's in the person of his double, and Raskolnikov's in the person of Svidrigaylov. In *The Eternal Husband* the guilty conscience of Velchaninov is incarnated in the person of Trusotsky, who has no common characteristics at all with Velchaninov. In the beginning of the story, Velchaninov appears to be suffering from the painful memory of his past. Brooding over his previous life, he lapses into a state of deep dejection. When he searches for the origin of his sudden anxiety and spiritual pain, he comes to the conclusion that it is all associated somehow with the inexplicable presence of a man with black crepe on his hat, a man whom he met by chance in the street some time ago. Velchaninov finds it impossible to connect his suffering in any logical manner with someone who is an apparent stranger, but the thought of him lingers in his mind. One night he is awakened from an obscure but tormenting dream by the loud ringing of the door bell. He rushes to the door, but there is no one there, and he finally convinces himself that it was only part of his dream. However, his agitation keeps him from sleep. Wandering across to the window, he sees his enemy down below, standing on the other side of the street, peering across at his house. Although Velchaninov does not even hear his steps, he knows that the stranger is coming to him, and divines his every movement through the closed door. It appears to Velchaninov that his dream has melted into reality, though he still cannot grasp the whole meaning of this mystery. Flinging the door open, he faces his nocturnal visitor. This dream-like confrontation, which is the projection of Velchaninov's irrational ego, finds its realistic foundation in the following scene. Trusotsky, the man with crepe on his hat, is neither a phantom nor a dream, but the husband of a woman with whom Velchaninov had a clandestine love affair some nine years before. This intrusion of Trusotsky may imply that only in his dream can Velchaninov find the courage to acknowledge the reason for his guilty conscience.

The symbolism of dreams is one of Dostoevsky's favorite expedients for the allegoric expression of his thoughts and convictions. Frequently these dreams represent symbolically the philosophical idea underlying the work in question.[16] The scope of this book, however, does not allow a detailed analysis of dreams, which depict the most significant stages in the spiritual development of his heroes. His remarkable achievements in this sphere deserve further special study.[17]

While in *The Idiot* and *The Eternal Husband* Dostoevsky concentrates mainly on the psychological issues, the philosophical implications become predominant in *The Possessed*. In his preceding works Dostoevsky appears to have entered into the minds of different people and seen the world around them from their point of view. He seems to have identified himself with their experiences and thoughts. In *The Possessed* Dostoevsky is rather an observer of events and people who symbolize certain ideas. The human "impulse of destruction," represented in *The Idiot* chiefly in its psychological aspect, is considered here more or less from the philsophical point of view. The irresistible power of the "impulse of destruction" becomes the core of Dostoevsky's concern and creative method. Stavrogin, the central character, who is conceived as an individual in the rational context of the novel, seems at the same time to personify evil on a symbolical level.

Stavrogin's nocturnal visit to his faithful disciples, Shatov and Kirillov, again illustrates Dostoevsky's employment of dream-logic. There are the dark and sodden gardens, the deserted streets; and into this scene of desolation comes Stavrogin, as if driven to his victims by his guilty conscience, just as Raskolnikov is driven to the house of the old money-lender after the murder. Although neither Shatov nor Kirillov has any logical reason to expect Stavrogin, they both know subconsciously that he will come, and show no surprise at his arrival. The sequence of scenes and their hidden symbolism, again, strongly resemble a dream. Stavrogin's conversations with both Shatov and Kirillov reveal his perilous influence upon them. The reader is here introduced to Kirillov's fanatical idea of "Man-become-God," which urges him to mount the empty throne of God through self-destruction. The scene with Shatov shows that his life is also endangered by his former absolute belief in the greatness of Stavrogin's political and social ideas.

Leaving Shatov, Stavrogin makes his way through the night to his wife's house. This scene is superbly designed to reflect the evil in Stavrogin's soul. It is a dark night, with the roaring wind tossing the bare tree-tops. His feet slip in the mud and before him lies "a wide, misty, empty, as it were, expanse," as if all life around him had become suddenly extinct. There is not a soul to be seen, until suddenly from the menacing darkness a man appears beside him. His shaggy hair is partly covered by a cloth cap with a half torn brim; his large eyes with their yellowish tinge have a hard glitter; and his whole physical appearance intensifies the impression of this dark portentous night. This stranger, the convict Fedka, offers to kill Stavrogin's wife, an offer which gives concrete expression to Stavrogin's covert desire to free himself from his crippled wife and marry Liza.

The scene which follows with Marya Timofeevna, Stavrogin's insane wife, resembles a delirious dream. With a look of horror, she lifts her trembling hands as if in defense, as she becomes conscious of Stavrogin's fixed and searching gaze, the expression of "a malignant enjoyment of her fright" in his eyes. Then, wishing to deceive her, he suddenly changes his grim facial expression into the "most cordial and amiable smile." Like Kirillov and Shatov, she temporarily succumbs to his deceptive charm, but now she keeps careful watch for any evil which may lurk beneath the amiable smile and caressing words. For a brief moment this scene seems to become Stavrogin's dream, giving him warning of his evil subconscious, the same warning sounded by Svidrigaylov's first appearance before Raskolnikov. As though gifted with clairvoyance, Marya Timofeevna obstinately addresses Stavrogin as "Prince," distinguishing him from another, true Stavrogin. "Is he alive?" she asks him, "Have you killed him? Confess!" Perceiving the true nature of Stavrogin, she refuses to see in him her beloved, her Prince, her "noble falcon." She recollects the dream which she had before Stavrogin entered the room, and considers it a dream no longer. "When you came in just now you took out your knife," she accuses him. With Marya Timofeevna's sudden exposure of his evil ego, Stavrogin sees before him his lost goodness and his present wicked and dissolute life. In panic he flees from her.

Dostoevsky employs dream-logic also in his last novel, *The Brothers Karamazov*. We can find it, for example, in the scene of Ivan's first conversation with Smerdyakov, when the two see through one another so well that they unmistakably read the thoughts and feelings of each other. The efforts of Ivan's suppressed ideas to struggle out of the obscurity of his unconscious mind, and the inability of his conscious mind to make contact with these intruding elements are given in great detail. Unable to bear the restless efforts of the unconscious to unburden itself, Ivan falls ill and meets in a hallucination his evil ego—his devil. In their subsequent arguments, dream and reality merge until Ivan's struggle against his hallucination finally exhausts his strength, and his personality loses its stability.

Like his predecessor, E. T. A. Hoffmann,[18] whose main interest, according to the studies made by C. G. Jung, was the problem of duality in human nature,[19] Dostoevsky in his novels avails himself of the technique of dream-logic as a mode of exploring chaotic conflicts in man. Using Freudian terms, we can describe these conflicts as the struggle between man's ego and super ego, his "subliminal self," [20] a theme which began to interest Dostoevsky already in the early phase of his literary career.

In *Bobok*, written in 1873, Dostoevsky is less concerned with depicting the depths of man's nature and the unconscious motives for his actions. Here he again concentrates on the philosophical issues: mankind cannot live without Christ, without a lofty moral ideal. As in *Crime and Punishment*, the line of demarcation between reality and dream is obliterated: it is difficult to determine whether the hero hears the muffled voices of the dead in a dream or in a waking state. Dostoevsky says explicitly that it happens in reality: "At first, I paid no attention, assuming a contemptuous attitude. Still, the conversation continued. I hear—the sounds are dull, as if the mouths are covered up with pillows; and at that —they are audible and seem quite close. I woke up and began listening intently." This picture of one of the most horrifying mystical experiences—the spiritual disintegration and moral corruption of the godless world—is given against the background of vividly realistic details: green water in the grave, every minute bailed out by the grave-digger with a scoop; a little restaurant, crowded by those attending the funeral; a half-eaten sandwich on a slab; and an elongated stone in the shape of a marble sepulchre.

Inherent in Dostoevsky's artistic method is this use of dream-logic by which he heightens the effect of the main themes and reveals hidden truths within the human soul. This technique imparts to his works their uncanny force and their persuasive power. It is this technique which so perfectly suits the author's artistic aim: to explain the unconscious, to disentangle and analyze the elements of man's spiritual life, and to expose remote metaphysical truths.

3　BIOGRAPHICAL FACTORS

DESPITE A NOTICEABLE TENDENCY among modern biographers and critics to represent and interpret Dostoevsky's childhood as a "hard childhood," [1] or an "unbearable life," [2] enough evidence indicates that Dostoevsky had a happy childhood. Some of these critics even go so far as to maintain that the novelist hated his father and felt a kind of physical repugnance for him.[3] Dostoevsky's brother, Andrey, however, stated in his account of Fyodor's life that his older brother thought about his parents with much gratitude and kindness. "Toward the end of the 1870's," Andrey Dostoevsky recalls, "I mentioned our father. My brother at once became animated, seized my arm above the elbow (this was his habit whenever he was engaged in a spirited conversation), and said with passionate conviction, 'Do you realize, brother, that our parents were progressive people, and they would be progressive even at this very moment! . . . We shall never be such parents, such fathers.'" [4] Dostoevsky's second wife, Anna Grigoryevna, remarked in her reminiscences that "Fyodor Mikhaylovich liked to evoke his peaceful happy childhood." [5] Karl Nötzel, a distinguished Dostoevsky scholar from Germany, whose book *Das Leben Dostojewskis* is based on twenty years' research in Russia, and who claims "to have had in [his] hands the whole of the Russian material" [6] on Dostoevsky, also asserts that the novelist's childhood was a happy one which stood in sharp contrast to his subsequent life at the

Military Engineers' Academy in St. Petersburg. The evaluation of Dostoevsky's childhood, thus, is open to discussion; and there appears to be some ground for believing that the sudden change in Dostoevsky's personal life after his arrival in St. Petersburg in 1837 had a depressing effect upon him, similar to the effect experienced by Gogol, whose glowing hopes were crushed by the impact of St. Petersburg reality.

Biographers almost unanimously agree that Dostoevsky's father at all times endeavored to remove unfavorable influences from his children's lives and spared no expense for their education and upbringing. Sometimes he was unreasonably strict, but he disliked giving his children moral admonitions and never resorted to corporal punishment. He is supposed to have taken every opportunity to teach and educate his children. The whole family adored the mother, a kind and sympathetic parent. When at Chermak's boarding school, before they entered the Military Engineers' Academy, Fyodor Dostoevsky and his brother Mikhail were treated as members of the Chermak family; they ate at the same table and, if ill, were cared for by Madame Chermak herself. On Saturdays, the brothers went home to a holiday meal of their favorite dishes. During this meal, they entertained their family with stories of their new life at school, and their father never reproved them even for their most daring escapades.

From this sheltered family existence, Dostoevsky entered the brutal world of the Military Engineers' Academy. He complained to Mikhail of his hateful life there, adding that he longed for beautiful things which were free from "earthly materialism." Filled with the lofty ideals of Homer, Schiller and Pushkin, Dostoevsky found this impact of the outside world a bitter experience. The physical hardship of the training, lack of money and particularly the uncongenial environment irked him. Referring to the time of study at the Academy, Dostoevsky said in *The Diary of a Writer*, "My brother and I were striving to begin a new life. Both of us were animated by a passionate belief in something, . . . yet while knowing full well that we were facing an examination in mathematics, we dreamt only of poetry and fiction." [7]

Upon his arrival at the Academy, Dostoevsky soon saw that his new life demanded far more than an examination in mathematics. As can be judged from the reminiscences of D. V. Grigorovich,[8] the cadets of the Engineers' Academy were ruthless and cruel youths. Dostoevsky always held himself aloof from his fellow students and their forms of amusement. Later, in *The Diary of a Writer*, he explained his attitude toward them. Here he noted that even at this early stage of their lives the cadets dreamt only "of well paid positions, worshipped only success in life and had nothing but a rude mockery for all those who were downtrodden." In *Notes from the Underground*, Dostoevsky wrote, "How dull they looked! In our school, the expression on the faces of the boys degenerated into brutishness. . . . At the age of sixteen I looked upon them with dismal surprise. I was amazed by the pettiness of their thoughts, games, conversations and pursuits. . . . They were accustomed to worship only success. . . . At the age of sixteen they already spoke of good little lucrative positions. . . . They were vicious to the point of monstrosity."

Dostoevsky's position at the Academy was made more difficult through shortage of money. His father sent him such a small allowance that he could not satisfy his barest needs; there was a time when he could not even afford tea. His distress is evident in his letter to his father: "I must, whether I wish or not, conform to the obligations of my immediate environment. Why should I be different? Such exceptional attitudes, moreover, are often attended by the greatest unpleasantnesses." [9] These lines indicate that Dostoevsky's pride and vanity suffered from these humiliations. Perhaps Devushkin's conviction that "one drinks tea because of one's neighbors" springs from Dostoevsky's own experience at the Academy.

The clash between Dostoevsky's ideals and reality, which became more overwhelming with the passing years, is reflected in a letter to his brother: "I do not know if my gloomy mood will ever leave me. To think that only such a state of mind is allotted to man: The atmosphere of his soul seems compounded of a mixture of the heavenly and the earthly. What an unnatural product, then, is man, since in him the law of spiritual nature is violated. . . . I feel that our world has become one immense Negative, and that everything noble, beautiful, and divine, has turned itself into a satire." [10]

In these reflections lies the kernel of Dostoevsky's philosophy, which he later elaborates so forcefully in his fiction. How is man, burdened with such conflicts, to fit into the world created by God? This was the beginning of Dostoevsky's journey into the dark land of man's duality. Man is created in the divine image; his spiritual striving is directed toward unification with God and eternity, yet his earthly desires impede these aspirations. Only the will to give up all earthly longings can free man's spirit and unify him with eternity. Dostoevsky expounded this thought in the same letter: "If in this picture there occurs an individual who neither in idea nor effect harmonizes with the whole—who is, in a word, an entirely detached figure—what must happen to the picture? It is destroyed, and can no longer endure. Yet how terrible it is to perceive only the coarse veil under which the All languishes! To know that one single effort of the will suffices to remove that veil and allow man to become one with eternity—to know all this, and still live on like the last and least of creatures. How terrible!" Man is too weak to remove this veil of matter which hinders his spirit in its pursuit of the ultimate goal.

This "coarse veil of matter" first intruded into Dostoevsky's life through his financial difficulties. Money worries distressed him particularly because his single-hearted enthusiasm for Schiller's high ideals and for Homer had hitherto crowded out almost all concern for mundane matters. Essentially impractical and improvident, he soon spent the small legacy left him by his father, and his life was then beset with anxiety. His difficulties were aggravated by the gambling frenzy he suffered while abroad. Dr. Riesenkampf, with whom Dostoevsky shared an apartment after he had abandoned his military career, wrote to Dostoevsky's brother, Mikhail, "Fyodor Mikhaylovich is constantly poor while his entourage lives in clover. They are pitilessly stripping him clean; he is one of those people who can never manage his finances. With his peculiar credulity, he will not have any search conducted in order to unmask his servants and their followers, who misuse his carelessness so badly." [11] Later in his life, Dostoevsky even voluntarily burdened himself with the debts of his deceased brother Mikhail and the support of Mikhail's legitimate and illegitimate children. He also financed his brother Nikolay and his own stepson Pavel Isayev. Dostoevsky assumed all these responsibilities with little consideration for his own financial difficulties. "With indignation I thought of all these idlers, because I saw that such constant financial worriers deprived Fyodor Mikhaylovich of his peaceful frame of mind and had a harmful effect on his health," [12] wrote Anna Grigoryevna.

A desperate letter from Geneva to Maykov of August 28, 1867, in which Dostoevsky confessed pawning his wife's last warm clothes, bears witness to the depth of misery caused by his lack of money. Throughout his life, Dostoevsky despised the bondage of money. His longing was to be free from concern over such worldly matters in order that he might live for the spirit. Money tormented him, Dostoevsky complained in a letter to Mikhail, since it belonged to that material sphere which impedes man's spiritual aspirations. Money was too insignificant, too trifling a matter to waste any thought upon, because thoughts, for Dostoevsky, belong to the region of the "heavenly." However, to secure the bare necessities of life, life itself forced him to sell those thoughts for money!

This clash of spirit versus matter intensified the internal conflict which first began when, filled with idealistic aspirations, he faced disappointing reality after his arrival in St. Petersburg. He now recognized the impossibility of living completely for the spirit while being forced to struggle for the means of existence. The "earthly bread," as the Grand Inquisitor later said, in most cases precedes the "heavenly bread," because man is too weak to change this order. The precariousness of human existence, in the Grand Inquisitor's eyes, is contained in the necessity for man to work for his daily bread. Man longs for union with others, "for the craving for universal unity is . . . the last anguish of man," says the Grand Inquisitor, but man is hindered in this by the need to earn his living, "for never, never will people be able to share among themselves!" The majority of people are not able "to forgo the earthly bread for the sake of the heavenly."

Dostoevsky's whole life was a tortured attempt to forgo the "earthly bread" for the sake of the "heavenly bread." It is apparent from his treatment of Luzhin (*Crime and Punishment*), Lambert (*A Raw Youth*), and Rakitin (*The Brothers Karamazov*), whose main concern in life is its material side, that Dostoevsky regarded money somewhat scornfully. Convinced that material wealth deprives man of freedom, he observed that

> The unruliness of desires only leads to slavery. That is why almost the whole contemporary world sees its freedom in financial well-being as well as in the laws which guarantee such material security. "If I have money it means that I can do whatever I like; with this money I shall neither perish nor ask anyone for help, which is the highest freedom." However [said Dostoevsky], this is not really freedom, but slavery, slavery imposed by money. The highest freedom is not found in financial security, but "in distributing all one has among others, and serving them all." If man is capable of such an action, capable of overcoming himself to such an extent, is it not he, then, who is free? This is the loftiest manifestation of freedom.[13]

This conviction establishes points of similarity with the philosophy of Tolstoy, who preached self-abnegation for the sake of others, with the individual sacrificing himself to the whole of humanity in which he duly dissolves.

Tolstoy taught that life should no longer be centered in the personality, but only in that universal Kingdom of God in which there is no division of any kind: no self-seeking, no private property, and therefore no friction, no struggle for mine and thine, but only harmony and brotherly love.

Dostoevsky himself could never shut out of his mind the gnawing thoughts of his own material distress—being forced to feed, clothe, and pay the debts of those dependent upon him. But he endowed some of his more fortunate heroes with this enviable and convenient faculty to overlook entirely their financial difficulties and apprehensions. Raskolnikov, although destitute and tortured by the knowledge of his mother's and sister's poverty, is simply unable to concentrate on such realities. He allows himself to be transported away from these difficulties by his dream of becoming a Titan who transgresses the law and destroys existing values. Shatov in *The Possessed*, also in financial difficulties, does not trouble himself with the question of money, but thinks of quite different matters. Versilov in *A Raw Youth* and Ordynov in "The Landlady" have no money, but their thoughts rarely turn to this subject. Arkady Dolgoruky in *A Raw Youth* longs for money only in order to free himself from matter. He wants to stand "on a solitary height," far away from troublesome people, with their tedious everyday problems, with whom he cannot cope. Dmitry Karamazov's hopeless attempts to obtain money to extricate himself from the ambiguous situation caused by his debt to Katerina Ivanovna give a striking illustration of Dostoevsky's fruitless desire "to remove the coarse veil and become one with eternity." Dmitry, whose strongest wish, as he says to Alyosha, is to sing hymns to glorify "God in the world and God in me," is placed by his father in such a situation that he is prepared to commit murder to procure money. Though he might long to revel in the ideal of purity, in the ideal of the Sistine Madonna, he is destined to end with the ideal of Sodom.

Dostoevsky's years of imprisonment defined and deepened his interest in the human soul. In his *Memoirs from the House of the Dead*, written after four harrowing years in Siberia, Dostoevsky portrays man as a spiritual being, even though burdened with base instincts. These instincts, present in man to a greater or lesser degree, sometimes overweigh his "heavenly" world but seldom eliminate it completely. "What a profound and enlightened human feeling, and what a refined, almost feminine, tenderness can dwell in the heart of some crude, bestially ignorant Russian peasants," [14] remarks Dostoevsky. In Siberia he discovered that among the convicts there were "wonderful people!" [15] Far from seeing them as mere wretches and outcasts, Dostoevsky optimistically described them as "the strongest, and, in one way or another, the most gifted of our people." [16]

Startled by this discovery, he began a metaphysical examination of good and evil in the human soul. He saw that the morbidly ambitious nature of the convicts sometimes resulted in a thwarted ego; they often lost sight of their real desires and became concerned only with impressing others with their superiority. In their behavior, Dostoevsky came to recognize man's wish to delude himself with an imaginary freedom. Some of them tried to postpone execution by the self-infliction of painful wounds, even though they knew they would be able only to defer the punishment, not escape it. They would rather endure great physical torments at their own hand than suffer at the will of authority. They suffered less from the exertions and privations of penal servitude than from the compulsion to work, which offended their sense of freedom. "I did not consider the work itself so hard," Dostoevsky wrote in *Memoirs from the House of the Dead*, "not at all as *forced* labor; and it was quite a while before I saw that the work was hard and *unbearable* not so much because of its difficulty and continuity, but mostly because of its *constraint*, obligation, and enforcement." This observation is further reflected in *Notes from the Underground*, where the hero remarks that "men love their own will and caprice more than profit." Man values his free will more than anything else. Strangely enough, this yearning for freedom exists side by side with man's fear to assume responsibility for his own actions and decisions. This theme is expanded in Dostocvsky's later works, particularly in "The Legend of the Grand Inquisitor."

In the behavior of the convicts, Dostoevsky also came to see man as a "mixture of the heavenly and the earthly." Speaking about Petrov, the novelist depicted him as a strong-willed and determined man, who, whenever he could, wholeheartedly helped Alexander Petrovich Goryanchikov, the supposed author of *The Memoirs*. His solicitous care was like that of a mother for her only child, without any thought of recompense. This tacit affection, however, did not prevent his stealing various articles, including a Bible, from Goryanchikov, in order to buy vodka; and this act was performed just as naturally as all the other things he undertook.

The years in Siberia also provided Dostoevsky with rich material for studying the type of man who can be dominated by his baser passions to such an extent that he may finally fall prey to spiritual disintegration. In his portrayal of Gazin especially, Dostoevsky showed man's delight in excesses of degradation, in iniquity, and in cunning.

These impressions of duality in human nature gradually come to the fore in other works of Dostoevsky. In *The Brothers Karamazov*, he states that a man is often ready to set his native village aflame and walk to Jerusalem as a pious pilgrim. In *The Eternal Husband*, he expresses the opinion that man, while embracing another with a genuine feeling of friendship, is still capable of murdering him; it is this duality which causes the final collapse of Ivan Karamazov, the intellectual instigator of a patricide. Torn between idealistic aspirations and sordid earthly desires, he finally suffers a mental breakdown.

On the psychological level, Dostoevsky's interest in man's dual nature was stimulated by contemporary studies of the relationship between the conscious and unconscious mind. His principal source of data on man's dissociated other self was Carl Gustav Carus's psychological study *Psyche zur Entwicklungsgeschichte der Seele*.[17] Published in 1846, it was based on G. H. v. Schubert's theories of animal magnetism.[18] Carus developed in great detail Schubert's observations on the curious interplay of conscious and unconscious states of mind into an impressive hypothesis of the "gradual emergence of consciousness from the unconscious." [19] It may well be supposed that Carus's book, written along romantic lines, guided Dostoevsky toward one of his favorite themes: the portrayal of half-formed emotional reactions emerging into the conscious mind.

Besides the study of Carus, Dostoevsky was familiar with the romantic writings of E. T. A. Hoffmann. This German novelist frequently portrayed characters with conflicting tendencies which often become incompatible and at last present themselves as separate and independent entities. Dostoevsky wrote to his brother Mikhail [20] that he was particularly interested in Hoffmann's story "Der Magnetiseur," in the artistic elaboration of the conflict between man's evil nature, with its magnetic power, and man's normal self, with its moral ideal. Alban, the evil hypnotist, overwhelms Marie's ideas and impulses to such an extent that she considers him a part, a higher intellectual and life-giving aspect, of her being. Medardus in *Die Elixiere des Teufels* experiences painfully the two distinct and alternate halves of his personality when his evil impulses are engaged in a dramatic duel with his conscious virtuous desires. When he gives way to the dominance of the former, he finds himself helplessly subjected to the power of an external and hypnotic mind. Another form of the double appears in Hoffmann's "Prinzessin Brambilla," where the writer shows characters, unable to withstand the dark powers of fate, collapsing and disintegrating. As a result of their disintegration, these heroes confront their "new selves," who are personified doubles or *Doppelgängers*. Giglio and Giacinta, hero and heroine of the tale, who manifest confused personalities and envisage a *Doppelgänger* as their "outside self," have no physical doubles before their eyes. They are subject to self-duplication, or multiplication.

Dostoevsky, using extensively Carus's psychological data, showed a striking affinity for Hoffmann's treatment of the *Doppelgänger*. In the case of Golyadkin and Ivan Karamazov, who confront their "other, new selves," emerging from their subsconscious, Dostoevsky, too, portrayed a process of mental collapse by means of a hallucinatory *Doppelgänger*. Ivan's devil appears before him as a concrete human being, and Ivan, like many of Hoffmann's characters, is unable at first to distinguish between hallucination and reality. Only later does he recognize and perceive in the devil his *Doppelgänger*, his evil self, the "lackey" in his nature. "You are a lie," Ivan says to his devil, "you are my illness, you are a phantom . . . you are my hallucination. You are the incarnation of myself, but only of one side of me . . . of my thoughts and feelings, only the nastiest and most stupid of them. . . . You just say what I am thinking . . . and are incapable of saying anything new."

Ivan's hallucinations are reminiscent of Stavrogin's vision of the devil, in the suppressed chapter of *The Possessed*. Stavrogin admits seeing an evil spirit, his evil self that becomes the *Doppelgänger*. "It is really I myself who appear in different forms!" he confesses to Tikhon. This evil self in Stavrogin's nature obtrudes from the conscious similarly to Medardus' partial self-projection. In *The Double* Dostoevsky showed an even greater likeness to Hoffmann's artistic methods. Golyadkin's "other, new self" appears as a true *Doppelgänger* in the Hoffmannesque sense of an identical person; and like Medardus, who considers Viktorin, his double, an enemy, Golyadkin also regards his *Doppelgänger* as a malignant foe, able to spy on Golyadkin's innermost thoughts and feelings and interfere with his personal intentions.

On the metaphysical level, Dostoevsky's preoccupation with the theme of duality was prompted, it may be supposed, by his epileptic attacks. Murin of "The Land-lady," Kirillov of *The Possessed*, Smerdyakov of *The Brothers Karamazov*, and Prince Myshkin of *The Idiot* all suffer from epilepsy. Through Prince Myshkin, Dosto-evsky represented the few seconds preceding an epileptic fit as a moment of supreme knowledge. "When I re-call and analyze this moment in a normal condition," Prince Myshkin reflects, "it seems to have been one of harmony and beauty in the highest degree—an instant of deepest sensation, overflowing with unbounded joy and rapture, reconciliation, ecstatic devotion, and the highest synthesis of life." About himself, Dostoevsky wrote the following to N. N. Strakhov: "For a few seconds, I experience such a happiness, one which is quite impossible in man's normal condition, and of which other people have no idea. I feel complete har-mony within myself and in the whole world, and this sensation is so strong and so sweet that I could imagine one giving away ten years of his life, probably his whole life, for a few seconds of this bliss." [21]

If Dostoevsky, during those instants prior to an attack, experienced "consciousness of self and an intense quicken-ing of the sense of personality" which reconciled him with everything existing, it would seem that he saw in this brief moment the universe, with the suffering of mankind, with man's sins and shortcomings, as the "highest har-mony and beauty." Duality must, then, have appeared to him beautiful, and a component part of beauty. "The awful thing is that beautiful is not only terrible but also mysterious. God and the devil are fighting there and the battlefield is the heart of man," observes Dmitry Kara-mazov.

A similar beauty may be found in the tragic fate of Svidrigaylov, who commits suicide because he sees no purpose in life. This beauty is dual because of his good deeds toward his youthful bride and Sonya Marmeladov and her relatives, on the one hand; and on the other, because of the full realization of his hopeless bondage to sin. Beauty is also found in the confession of Stavrogin, who, while he indulges in vice and depravity, can, at the same time, dream of the harmony of the Golden Age.

It is a striking fact that the characters of Dostoevsky who are subject to epilepsy are diverse types of people with little in common. There is the mysterious Murin with the qualities of the evil demon, the Christlike Prince Myshkin, the servile Smerdyakov, and the noble-minded Kirillov. It may be suggested that Dostoevsky either united within himself these dissimilar characteristics, or that he tended to interpret this malady as a sign that evil, too, belongs to the universal harmony which he experienced for brief moments with rapture and clarity. Dostoevsky's avowal of dual tendencies in his own nature could be taken as a premise for the first supposition,[22] while the second may be based on an observation by Stepan Trofimovich Verkhovensky in *The Possessed*. Shortly before his death, he tells Varvara Petrovna that "the Infinite and the Eternal are as essential for man as the little planet on which he dwells. . . . Hail the Great Idea! The Eternal, Infinite Idea! It is essential that every man, whoever he may be, bow down before the Great Idea!" Stepan Trofimovich believes that all men, even the evil ones, belong to that Eternal and Infinite Idea. From this and the later *Diary of a Writer*, it becomes clear that the great idea is God and immortality, of which every man partakes. It is for the sake of this participation in the idea of God and immortality that Dostoevsky always saw innate goodness in men, however evil they may have appeared to others. We may conclude that, in all likelihood, Dostoevsky's illness contributed to his perception of man as a dual being.

A further motive inducing Dostoevsky to take up the problem of duality in man, as well as in the structure of the world, may be found in the Russian thought of the period. Dostoevsky's views of Russia's cultural, ideological, and economic development resembled, and were influenced by, the tenets of the two antithetical schools of literary and political thought, the Slavophils and Westernizers. He agreed with the Slavophils that Russia, infused with true Christianity and deep feeling, had a historic mission of redeeming Europe from the rationalism, materialism, and egoism which weakened her stability. He shared the enthusiasm of the Westernizers for the reforms of Peter the Great, but sharply opposed their fundamental conviction that Russia was to imitate the West, and attacked their failure to emphasize the significance of religion and spirituality.

Dostoevsky loved Russia and, like many other educated Russians of the time, considered himself and his country to be an integral part of Western civilization. "To the Russian," says Versilov, "Europe is as precious as Russia. . . . Europe is as much our fatherland as Russia. Oh, even more so. No one could love Russia more than I do, but I have never reproached myself that Venice, Rome, Paris, the treasures of their arts and sciences, their whole history, are dearer to me than Russia." In the volume of *The Diary of a Writer*, published during the Russo-Turkish War, Dostoevsky wrote, "We cannot separate ourselves from Europe. Europe is our second home. I am the first to confess it with all my heart, and I have always done so. Europe is *almost* as dear to *all* of us as is Russia herself. Europe contains all the Aryan people, and our idea is the unity of all these nations." [23] Yet on the other hand, as N. Zernov points out, "Dostoevsky was disgusted by the cult of egoism among individuals and nations in the West; he deplored the exclusive preoccupation with material comfort and the acquisition of wealth among the European people." [24]

This dual attitude is also characteristic of Dostoevsky's complicated ideas concerning the European influence upon Russia. While he wholeheartedly accepted the ruthless and vigorous reforms of Peter the Great and held that they were propitious for Russian technological, economic, and scientific advances, he contended that the new ideas developed by Western political thought were harmful for Russia in her adherence to national cultural tradition. The new ideas and the flow of foreign life were so intoxicating to the Russian upper classes that the ties with the cultural and historical traditions of the past were gradually severed. Large sections of the Russian aristocracy looked upon the decline of old values without misgivings and with a calm detachment. They disdained the cultural past of their country, advocated the latest modes of life and thought in Europe, and underestimated Russia's indigenous culture and civilization.

This usurping of Russia's tradition disheartened Dostoevsky. He was disturbed by the thought that Russia, having her own individual intellectual and cultural development, which differed from that of the West, would be forced to assimilate European influences without having passed through all the developmental stages in succession. In such characters as Stavrogin, Stepan Trofimovich Verkhovensky and his son Pyotr, and Versilov among others, Dostoevsky showed that the assimilation of European ideas and doctrines alien to the nature of the Russian caused a spiritual split of the personality. It could only have an adverse effect, he considered, because the moral strength of Western Europe was extraneous to Russia. This moral strength, Dostoevsky believed, was a nation's concept of good and evil, its individual notion of God, which necessarily differed with each nation. The novelist wrote in his *Diary of a Writer*,

> The European nations strive for the same goal, they all have one and the same ideal, no one will deny this. However, their local interests divide them. Their exclusiveness even among themselves tends to extremes; and the more their separation intensifies, the more they neglect to strive for their common goal. . . . Their antagonism, robbing them of all unprejudiced ideas and notions, makes them biased. They cease to understand each other. . . . Their mutual separation in morals, habits and customs, as well as in the belief that the world is God's creation, becomes still more persistently and obstinately intense. . . . Each of them wants to accomplish for himself alone that which can be accomplished only by united nations, with their united strength. . . . Is their civilization, then, really so powerless that it cannot, even now, overcome their old hatred? . . . The Christianity which has been holding

them together until now, loses power each day. Nor can science unite them while they strive for individual lives.[25]

Dostoevsky's pessimism resulted from his mistrust of the spirit of the Roman Catholic Church. As he pointed out in his "Legend of the Grand Inquisitor," the Roman Catholic Church denied freedom, craved power and authority, and was ready at any time to compromise with evil, if such a compromise promoted immediate success and advantage. The Grand Inquisitor in "The Legend," a passionate idealist, is eager to relieve man of his burden of conscience, for in this he sees the only opportunity for man to find peace and tranquillity. Dostoevsky claimed that the godless spirit of the West and its revolt against spiritual freedom were generated by the Roman system, which insisted on absolute obedience and surrender to authority, even when these were at variance with the voice of conscience. He was convinced, therefore, that the Roman Catholic Church could not redeem Europe from the scepticism and rationalism which undermined her vitality, nor could it succeed in the procreation of friendship, mutual understanding, and co-operation among the European countries. Only the Russian people were mature to fulfill such an important task because of the Russian Orthodox interpretation of Christianity, with its true spirituality and deep religious feeling: "The Russian soil, the genius of the Russian people, is perhaps more capable than any other of incorporating the idea of universal union, of brotherly love and of a realistic outlook. . . . It forgives those who differ and resolves contradictions." [26]

Dostoevsky considered this universalism and brotherly love to be marked characteristics of the Russian interpretation of Christianity, which is rooted in another distinguishing feature of Russian mentality—freedom from fear of suffering. With their understanding of the meaning of spiritual pain, the Russians are not afraid to suffer. They accept the hardest of all trials because these secure the growth and maturity of one's personality. Dostoevsky further claimed that the readiness and the ability of the Russian people to face and endure suffering with fortitude and meekness would enable them to initiate a close relationship with other European countries. They are able to assimilate the flow of foreign life with their hearts and minds.

In Dostoevsky's opinion, while the West became increasingly alienated from the basic idea of Christianity—the unification of mankind through brotherly love—the Russians, with their acceptance of God and their fellow men, came nearer to achieving such a spiritual goal. Versilov, speaking of the new Russian, states, "Among us has been created a type of the highest culture such as has never been seen before and exists nowhere in the world. A type of human being with a compassion that embraces the world. It is a Russian type." Here we have described the type of man who, Dostoevsky fervently believed, would bring unity and harmony to the world.

Dostoevsky's notebooks give additional evidence of his firm belief that only his country could bring about Europe's spiritual rebirth: "Pray to God," he writes, "that He gives you more Russian thoughts. Your prayer must be heard by Him." [27] Dostoevsky's faith in the great moral capacities of the Russian people is expressed with even greater force in the following two entries: "Incalculate into [your] soul the belief that the truth is in the Russian soil and that its banner flies high . . . and then much of what you do not expect, do not see, and even do not imagine, will take place." [28] "We, the Russians, are bringing to the world the renewal of the ideal which has been lost to it." [29]

In Dostoevsky's concept of Russia's historic mission, we may perceive, without much difficulty, a reflection of the dualism projected both in the characters and in the ideas of his novels. For him, mankind is divided into the peoples of the West, who will support an ideal of unification through force, pride, and self-will; and the peoples of the East, who will attain their ideal of universal service through humility, love, and understanding. Dostoevsky's dual attitude toward Europe—his hostility toward her supposedly distorted and twisted Christianity, and his love for her because her past became Russia's past—augmented his philosophical interpretation of duality as the moving force of mankind.

All these revelations of duality, on the psychological and philosophical planes, were factors which induced Dostoevsky to take up the theme of man's duality in an attempt to find some justification for it.

4   SYMPTOMS OF SPIRITUAL DECAY

A MAIN CONCERN in Dostoevsky's fiction is the moral decay of the individual which springs from the neglect of his spiritual being. The dominance of man's animal nature, Dostoevsky warns, invariably leads to the debasement of the divine image within man and to his pollution as a spiritual entity. While describing the suffering of the egocentric hero as a natural result of his self-indulgence, Dostoevsky also depicts the suffering caused to those at whose expense the ego-centered character seeks to increase his own self-esteem. In his study of egocentricity, the novelist skilfully exposes the close interlacing of significant aspects of man's creaturely being: ambition, vanity, striving for superiority and domination, shame and its logical consequence, isolation. Presented in their complex entanglements, these manifestations of the natural being bear witness to the tragedy which ensues from man's duality.

All living things fulfill their purpose by assuming their intended place in the great harmony of God's creation. In this harmony man appears to be the only disturbing element, the only creature who fails to recognize in himself an organic part of the universe; thus he isolates himself from God and his fellow men. This is the concept of man put forth by Dostoevsky in his novels. Instead of living according to Christ's teaching that all men are brothers, Dostoevsky's egocentric hero seems often to be guided in his life by Hobbes's viewpoint that *homo homini lupus est*. The physical and spiritual worlds of man stand in opposition to each other. His desire for ego-gratification isolates him from nature and from his fellows to such an extent that he is unable to comprehend, even less to lead, the spiritual life. In his attempts to fulfill this desire, his "divine countenance becomes distorted into a human—much too human—face." [1]

Frequently in Dostoevsky's works, a man separated from the "harmony of the universe," and thus bereft of his purpose in life as a spiritual being, indulges in the gratification of his natural self. This promotes in him the ambition to assume a role which sets him above others and gives him power over them. He recognizes only his own ego; the world becomes a competitive field and his fellow men his opponents. In seeking superiority over others, he is forced to conceal his shortcomings and to feign virtues which he does not really possess. He considers that men succumb more readily to the influence of a person who enjoys high esteem in society, so he seeks to make others believe that he is endowed with all the virtues which are respected by them. This is often difficult, for his fellows, aware of their own limitations and base instincts, are quick to recognize these same qualities in others. Their own egos supply the standard for all judgment, for as Dmitry Karamazov puts it, "Nobody is able to judge except by taking himself as a standard." Consequently, they are able to detect the weaknesses which lie beneath the egocentric hero's veneer of virtue. Finally time proves to him that his hopes for power, influence, and glory can never be realized, because others recognize his shortcomings; when this occurs, he withdraws into the seclusion of his own self.

Dostoevsky's apprehensions over the human trait of vanity find their reflections in the modern individual psychology of Alfred Adler, who says,

> Quite beside the fact that vanity leads an individual to all kinds of useless work and effort which is more often concerned with the *semblance* of things than with their *essence*, and beside the fact that it causes him to think

constantly of himself or at least only of other people's opinion of him, its greatest danger is that it leads him sooner or later to lose contact with reality. He loses his understanding for human connections; his relations in life become warped. He forgets the obligations of living, and loses sight especially of the contributions which nature demands of every man.[2]

Vain individuals attempt "to maintain at all costs their feeling of superiority, and to shield their vanity from any insult." "The vain one always knows how to shift the responsibility for any mistakes to the shoulders of another. He is always right; the others are always wrong." And what is more, "Vanity is forced to hide itself, . . . disguise itself, and make detours to accomplish its end." [3]

Dostoevsky's concern with vanity and its distortion of human nature can be traced throughout his works. With *The Double,* he begins to develop the theme of duality as an evil manifestation of man's creaturely being. Golyadkin, a simple, ordinary and rather wretched man, has only one ambition: to gain the acceptance and admiration of his colleagues and superiors. He seeks their respect through flattery, intrigues, and the affectation of social graces. This proves futile, however, as his colleagues, discerning these obvious pretensions, are not impressed. This failure changes his entire attitude. He now boasts that he is a man who acts "openly and without subterfuge," loathes slander and gossip, and "wears a mask only at a masquerade." "I do not act surreptitiously," he declares to Krestyan Ivanovich, "but openly and without any ruses; and although I could harm others in turn, and how well I could do this, I do not wish to stain myself with such deeds." He now tries to suppress the desire to achieve the status of his superiors by maintaining self-righteously that his own position is just as good as that of anyone else, and that, in his opinion, he is no worse than others. However, these assertions are only self-delusions: a longing for power, though submerged, still persists, and his determination to assert himself grows daily.

Since his interests do not extend beyond the circle of his colleagues, a circle which represents his social ideal, he longs for a position similar to that of Andrey Filippovich, his immediate superior. He persuades himself that "he is just as independent as anyone else," and just as able to live in Andrey Filippovich's grand style. To prove this to himself, Golyadkin goes to the fashionable emporiums of the Gostiny Dvor, where indiscriminately he buys anything he happens to espy, from cigarette-cases and tea sets to furniture. With no hope of ever paying for these purchases, he still promises to collect them the next day. Throughout this escapade he is quite conscious that he is merely imitating Andrey Filippovich, and "for nothing in the world would he agree now to meet his superior." Such an encounter would show him too clearly the difference in their social positions. But even with this realization Golyadkin is still eager to prove to himself that "he is just as independent as anyone else." A party which Andrey Filippovich is to attend presents a new opportunity, and Golyadkin goes there uninvited. When he is turned out as an intruder, he discovers that he has failed again, and that social success is not for him. He now fears some form of retribution from Andrey Filippovich for his unauthorized arrival at the party, and is afraid that future recollection of this attempt will rob him of the last remnants of his self-respect. His agony is intensified by the awareness that he does not belong to the beau monde.

As his only desire is the gratification of his ambitious ego, a gratification no longer possible, he may now either lapse into apathy, or commit suicide—the fate of several of Dostoevsky's characters. In Golyadkin's case, the writer chooses to show how strong the instinct for self-preservation is in a man of this type: Golyadkin finds a way out of his dilemma by refusing to regard his vanity as his own. He wishes now to forget his appearance at the party and to believe that he never had an urge for identification with Andrey Filippovich. "It is not I at all," he reflects, "really not. . . . He is a different man; he is a person to himself; and I am a person to myself." He now wishes to be a pliant and straightforward man, and attempts to suppress those impulses which are inconsistent with his new ideal. Through this attempt, his aspirations to be equal to his superiors grow even stronger and finally overwhelm him. He can no longer restrain his desires; they appear before him in the form of another being, who rises against him. The double is an intriguer, a hypocrite, and an unscrupulous careerist, an incarnation of all which Golyadkin no longer allows himself to be. He struggles with his double and tries to appease him. He is prepared to renounce his selfishness entirely and even to degrade himself before the double. Such degradation is a torment to Golyadkin's ego. The double, however, proves the stronger; Golyadkin is defeated, driven to despair, and finally taken to an insane asylum.

How seriously Dostoevsky is concerned with the theme of human selfishness and its resultant suffering can best be seen from a statement in *The Diary of a Writer*. Here, he acknowledges the fact that *The Double* was not enthusiastically received by his contemporaries, but he himself, he says, had always regarded its theme as most significant: "Most decidedly, I did not succeed with that novel . . . but I have never expressed anything more serious in my writings." [4]

The drive for ego gratification, which engenders only suffering, is portrayed in many of Dostoevsky's works, but such a human void as Golyadkin appears only once more as a central figure. This is Foma Fomich, in *The Village of Stepanchikovo*, a vain man, intent only on attaining power and admiration. In this novel Dostoevsky illustrates the effect of an egocentric person on the lives of others. Foma differs from Golyadkin inasmuch as he succeeds in fulfilling his desires, but this is only because of the weaknesses, misguided kindness, and stupidity of his neighbors. Two persons enable Foma to achieve his position in the house of the Krakhotkins. One is a sincere and good-natured colonel, free of any ambition and vanity, who in his foolish kindness succumbs voluntarily to

Foma's control. The other person is the colonel's mother, old, stupid, and capricious, who needs such a man as Foma through whom she in turn can impose her own will on others. In her stupidity, she attributes to Foma qualities of spiritual and intellectual greatness to which he has no claim whatever.

Foma enters General Krakhotkin's household as a sponger, but by feigning virtues and abilities highly respected by Mrs. Krakhotkin, he soon acquires influence over the female part of the household. "He read aloud to them works of spiritual edification; held forth with eloquent tears on Christian virtue; told stories of his life; at times foretold the future; had a peculiar faculty for interpreting dreams, and was a great hand at throwing blame on his neighbors." He is for Dostoevsky simply an "incarnation of unbounded vanity—the vanity found in a complete non-entity—whose most urgent craving is somewhere and somehow to stand first, to be an oracle, to swagger and give himself airs." He is the man Golyadkin aspired to be: a hypocrite, an intriguer, and a careerist.

In Foma's case the observation made by Adler concerning the vain attempt to dominate others is particularly appropriate:

> Vain people who would like to rule others must first catch them in order to bind them to themselves. . . . The first phase of this battle must be to assure one's opponent and cajole him so far that he loses his caution. In the first phase, that of friendly approach, one is easily tempted to believe that the aggressor is an individual with a great deal of social feeling; the second serves to remove the veil from our eyes and to show us our error. . . . We believe that they [vain people] have two souls, but it is but the one soul, which makes an amiable approach, but effects a bitter ending.[5]

Once Foma has successfully bound his neighbors to himself, he begins to tyrannize them ruthlessly, now giving free rein to his selfish desires, which finally sever him from reality and deprive him of meaning in life.

In *The Double* and *The Village of Stepanchikovo*, comes the initial warning that a man must be at least honest with himself and acknowledge his weaknesses, lest isolation become his sorry fate and his ego his tiny cosmos. Moreover, with the person of Foma, Dostoevsky implies for the first time that all are responsible for the sins of others, a deeply felt conviction which is fully developed in his later works. A vain man cannot make his way without the assistance of his fellows. He requires daily, and almost hourly, evidence of unlimited power over them, and the assurance that he is the center of their attention. He takes revenge on those whose attentions toward him become divided or incomplete, and redoubles his tyranny in order to become once again the focal point of their lives. Foma's friends suffer immensely from this tyranny, for they have to arrange their lives according to his selfish demands and expectations.

The theme of vanity is pursued further in "An Unpleasant Predicament." Pralinsky is a vain man, and in his selfishness he is determined, like Golyadkin and Foma, to indulge his ambitions. Just as Foma resembles Golyadkin, except for his success in achieving power over his associates—and this with their assistance—so Pralinsky resembles Foma except for those positive qualities which for the most part render constant evidence of his popularity and high position superfluous. Pralinsky, too, would like to rise above others and be respected and admired. He believes that one day "he will be not only a great dignitary, but a statesman whom Russia will long remember"; he even dreams of monuments erected in his honor. In particular, he hopes to gain advancement through his humane attitude toward his subordinates, through a new and promising idea that all people should "embrace each other in a moral sense." He realizes that his wish originates in vanity, but this does not hinder him from attempting to fulfill it. His colleagues, with whom he discusses his intentions, warn him that he will fail because his wish does not come from the heart, but from the mind, which desires only to promote personal interests;

they are unable, however, to dissuade him from pursuing his great idea.

An opportunity for Pralinsky to manifest his humanity soon presents itself. While passing the house of a subordinate, Pseldonimov, who is celebrating his wedding, Pralinsky decides to surprise him pleasantly by his unexpected arrival. This is to be the beginning of his popularity. Filled with a strong desire to love everyone, even those who he knows wish him ill, Pralinsky "suddenly longs to forget everything, and to embrace and be reconciled with everybody." He expects that the host, having overcome an initial shock, will "tremble with delight" over Pralinsky's "act of heroic virtue," but to his chagrin he soon notices that the effect is quite different. Placed in an embarrassing situation and forced outwardly to demonstrate devotion to his superior, Pseldonimov begins almost to hate him. Pralinsky's self-respect is deeply wounded by the hostile attitude of his host and the guests; and finally he is compelled to admit that he has gained only ridicule from an "embrace in a moral sense."

Golyadkin and Foma, seeking personal gratification, lie to themselves, but Pralinsky, who knows full well the real nature of his desires, wishes only to disguise them. He even acknowledges his defeat, for there still remains his elevated position with a certain degree of power and influence, and a hope that "his name will be long remembered in Russia" through some other great accomplishment. His idea of the "embrace in a moral sense" fails because his subordinates, who are not so unselfish, kind and narrow-minded as those who surround Foma, refuse to assist him in pursuing his vain goal. Though of much lower rank and social standing than Pralinsky, they are of much the same nature and, therefore, highly suspicious of his actions.

Pralinsky suffers terribly when he senses that the people around him recognize his vain intentions. "For eight days," Dostoevsky relates, "he did not leave the house or show himself at the office. He was ill, agonizingly ill, but more morally than physically. He lived through a real hell in those days, which must have been reckoned to his account in the other world." Since his desire for a "moral embrace" springs from egoism rather than from an idealistic love for mankind, as his colleagues point out, his ambition brings only suffering to himself and his fellow men. Pseldonimov, beset by complications arising from Pralinsky's presence at the wedding breakfast, is so anguished that he is brought almost to the brink of despair. "He fell into a leaden, deathlike sleep," says Dostoevsky of him, "such as must be the sleep of a man condemned to be flogged on the morrow." This statement reveals the depth of Pseldonimov's suffering as a result of Pralinsky's thoughtless ambition and vanity.

The theme of *Notes from the Underground* is again human vanity, but the hero is ready at any time to acknowledge unsparingly all his weaknesses, especially his egoism and vanity. While Golyadkin and Foma are tormented mainly because of their self-deception, the Underground Man suffers because of his self-knowledge. This makes him suspicious of himself and deprives him of the courage necessary to become a "man of action." Deeply conscious of his personality, he is an astute logician in explaining its complex nature. A morbid awareness of the contradictions in his character, a character which has been distorted by the dominance of his creaturely being, appears to be the whole history of the Underground Man, the entire substance of his searching intellect.

In this novel, Dostoevsky is not so much concerned with the suffering caused to others by a self-centered person, as in the case of Foma and Pralinsky, but directly with the the ego-centered personality itself. The suffering of the Underground Man therefore is deeper than that of the earlier characters. His egotism appears to him as an abominable and repulsive illness, and he introduces himself to the reader with utmost candor, "I am a sick man . . . I am a wicked man. I am an unpleasant man." There is very little trace of self-deception in his nature, and he wants to see himself as he really is. With his clear recognition that he is not a "great man," he does not take pride, as does Golyadkin, in being an "insignificant man." He realizes that he is a person whom people neither notice nor despise, too insignificant even for the concern of others. "I have never succeeded in being anything at all," he writes in his memoirs, "whether wicked or good-natured, a villain or an honest man, a hero or an insect. Now I am spending the rest of my days in my corner, scoffing and calling myself wicked, comforting myself with the entirely useless consolation that an intelligent man cannot seriously become anything, for only a fool does that. Yes, a man of the nineteenth century, for the most part, is morally bound to be a weak-willed man. Apropos of this—a man with character and a man of action must be essentially limited."

The Underground Man is convinced that an intelligent man, with his logic and insight, cannot become an "active man." An "active man," he thinks, can succeed only through self-deception. As a result of this knowledge, he develops strong inferiority feelings, for he can be "either a hero, or the dust-heap, anything but mediocrity." Throughout his life, he wallows in the hopeless contradictions of his personality: in his heart he yearns for respect from people whom he secretly despises; while dreading humiliation, he seeks it. Afraid to appear stupid and ridiculous, he prefers to have other people see viciousness in his face, "providing that they find it at the same time extremely intelligent." He so desires to stop playing a secondary role scorned by everyone, that he would rather live a life of corruption or withdraw into his underground than impress others as spiritually empty. Sometimes, when a sordid round of dissipation ends, he wishes to escape into "the great and the beautiful," to become a hero, and "to appear in God's world, mounted on a white horse and crowned with laurels." His experiences at the dinner given by his schoolmates for one of their friends, and in the bawdy house, are vivid illustrations of the actual workings of the Underground Man's dual nature. His vanity robs him of every opportunity to lead a positive existence, yet he refuses to accept the understanding friendship of Liza, a well-meaning prostitute. He must remain superior to her; he must make her suffer in order to assert his own self; he must be able to exercise power over her. "Power, power over someone, is what I want!" he cries when Liza visits him.

After she has gone leaving him a prey to the baseness of his soul, he is almost distraught, "I felt hardly alive because of the pain in my soul. Never before nor since have I suffered or repented so much as I did then," he says later. He does not beseech Liza to stay with him, for he knows that he will without fail take revenge on her for his own weakness, for the sense of power it gives him. In the confusion of cross-purposes he retreats into himself and vents his spite upon all and sundry. The origin of his suffering is egocentricity, the desire to achieve power over others; his awareness of both his wish to become a hero and the impossibility of ever appearing one heightens his anguish.

Dostoevsky's concept of the dual force whereby man is made to strive but doomed to fail is discernible in his treatment of the Underground Man. The Underground Man, too, is a victim of the universal force which strives toward an end and simultaneously denies that end. This force has produced in him a being with a keen intellectual awareness, imbued with the desire to strive for "something quite different," as he himself admits. However, instead of remaining faithful to this aim, he is repelled by the negative aspect of the force, the one denying the human goal. The precariousness of man's existence on the face of God's creation is shown by Dostoevsky here with great clarity. As his hero maintains, man can avail himself, so long as he has not attained a high level of intellectual awareness, of the opportunity to strive for it. Once he has reached it, he is driven to despair by his realization that the creaturely aspect of his being will prevent him from ever attaining this "something quite different." Finding himself in what appears to be a blind alley, the Underground Man begins to rage against himself. Unable to develop any positive qualities within himself, he cannot attune himself to the "spiritual world," and consequently cannot strive for "something quite different." It seems to him that he is removed from the stream of life by his profound understanding of his fellow men and of the world's structure. Therefore his words "I swear to you that to be conscious of too much is a malady, a real and complete malady" are born of tormenting personal experience. Unlike his predecessors, the Underground Man is an intellectual, yet his tragedy also hinges on his dual nature, on the dominance of his creaturely being.

The extreme form of this dominance is symbolically shown through the allegory in the short story "The Crocodile." Ivan Matveich, the hero of the story, does not seek to transform his vain ideas into actions, but formulates them into sterile theories which never go beyond the imagination.

In his later works, Dostoevsky gives a still deeper analysis of the human psyche, with ever-increasing emphasis on the distortion which springs from deception and falsity. He places ambition at the heart of the novel *Crime and Punishment*. Raskolnikov has certain characteristics in common with Dostoevsky's earlier heroes. Like them, he is concerned with vanity, or as he himself terms it, with his "flesh and lust." He has pride, too, but in him it produces quite different results. It spares him the torturing preoccupation with his personal insignificance, so characteristic of the Underground Man. It also enables him to dispense with the pretensions and feigned virtues of Golyadkin, Foma, and Pralinsky. Raskolnikov attempts to develop the actual moral and intellectual qualities which should aid his striving for self-assertion and the gratification of his ego. Most of all, he desires power over himself, not over others as do Foma and Pralinsky. This is a quality for which the Underground Man, although he makes no secret of his vanity, has neither the courage nor the moral strength. Raskolnikov wants to promote his career by exercising his will, and is prepared to discard all respect for fundamental human laws, as he believes his idol Napoleon to have done before him. He develops this theme in an article in which he claims the existence of "ordinary" and "extraordinary" people. "The first category," he writes, "preserves the world and increases its number; the second moves the world and leads it to its goal." "Ordinary" people have to obey the existing laws; "extraordinary" people create them and have a right to transgress them with impunity. "In the name of the better future," they "destroy the present" and have a moral right "to step over a corpse or wade through blood," for they are the "masters of the future." Raskolnikov's ambition is to become such an "extraordinary" man, another Napoleon.

In Raskolnikov's opinion, man must refuse to succumb to the limitations imposed on him by nature, and even rise above them with the will of a Titan. Man has every right to ignore existing laws; he must, therefore, cease to exist as the "unnatural product," which has transformed "the noble spiritual world into a satire," for even "one single effort of his will" may suffice to tear away the "coarse veil." [6] "If a man isn't really a beast . . . then all the rest is just prejudice, just imagined fears; there is nothing to stop you from doing anything you like, and that is as it should be," says Raskolnikov to himself. He makes up his mind to kill an old money-lender for whose existence he can find no justification. At this stage he rationalizes his decision simply as a desire to help his mother and sister and to finish his studies at the university.

On the eve of the murder he has a dream which shows him the selfishness of those who think only of their own convenience and pleasure. He dreams of a weak and defenseless mare being tortured to death by some peasants. Some of the onlookers experience mirth at the sight of its agony, others are indignant; but no one does anything to help the poor beast. Even Raskolnikov's father, who abhors these atrocities and genuinely pities the suffering animal, says to his son, "They are drunk . . . It is not our business. Come along!" After this dream Raskolnikov realizes that the motive he had fabricated for the murder is a self-deception, and that in reality it is the desire for gratification of his ego that urges him to kill the old woman. This egoism is similar to that which makes the drunken peasants torture the animal, and which prompts his father to say, "It is not our business. Come along!" However, Raskolnikov's self-love is stronger than any compunction awakened by this revelation, and thus he continues to strive for the gratification of his "flesh and lust." He primarily desires to prove to himself that he belongs to the category of "extraordinary" people, and that he is not a "louse" and a "scoundrel" unconditionally dependent upon the laws created for him by others, and upon the restrictions imposed on him by nature.

Soon after the murder, Raskolnikov understands that he was mistaken about himself. He discovers that he does not belong to the category of "extraordinary" people. His repulsive murder of the old woman and his search for valuables hidden in a box under her bed appear to him loathsome and unworthy of a Napoleon, whose exalted and noble achievements he had admired. He is haunted by the ugliness of his deed. Would a Napoleon have stooped to such an ugly and unheroic murder? He fears that now people will despise him because of his odious deed. He tortures himself with thinking, "Napoleon, the pyramids, Waterloo, and a skinny repulsive old hag, a money-lender with a red box under her bed, how could a man like Porfiry Petrovich stomach it! . . . Their aesthetic sense would not allow it: 'Would a Napoleon crawl under an old woman's bed?' Oh rot! . . ." He is now fully aware of the fact that he killed the old woman solely for personal gratification: "I simply killed her; I did it for myself, for myself alone!" This thought brings him such suffering that he falls ill "from wounded pride." Like Pralinsky, he admits he has failed, and even contemplates suicide, but his wish for punishment is stronger. Self-humiliation becomes an indispensable pleasure. "Yes, I am really a louse," he goes on, clinging to the idea with malicious delight, "I am a louse, because I myself am perhaps worse and nastier than the louse I killed, and I knew *beforehand* that I would say that to myself *after* killing her."

Raskolnikov is too honest to shift his responsibility onto others or to vent the fury caused by his feeling of inferiority upon them, as Golyadkin wishes to do and Foma, in fact, does. He cannot, however, refrain from torturing Sonya after his defeat. Later he reproaches himself: "Oh, how low I have sunk! No, what I wanted was her tears! What I wanted was to see her terror, to see how her heart ached and bled!" With this realization, he experiences a tormenting feeling of self-hate and a longing to take revenge against himself: "How did I dare, knowing myself, to take an axe in my hand and cover myself with blood! I ought to have known it beforehand. Oh, but I did! I did know beforehand!"

Unable to continue struggling with his conscience, he lapses into a state of apathy. His life stretches before him, barren and futile. In Dostoevsky's words, there is nothing "but senseless and aimless anxiety in the present, and in the future a life of self-sacrifice which would bring him nothing in return; that was what his whole life would be like." As his previous concern in life was the indulgence of his ambitious ego, his existence now loses all meaning for him, and he voluntarily turns himself in to the police; he has no wish to delude himself. At this stage he does not understand that his voluntary confession brings him one step nearer to the spiritual life, that his surrender "could be a turning point in his future life, in his future resurrection, in his new view of life." Raskolnikov is the first of Dostoevsky's heroes who, though at first completely engrossed in his "flesh and lust," succeeds in his "gradual transition from one world to another," and in making "his acquaintance with a new, hitherto unknown reality." He is the first to achieve the synthesis of the soul that will bring peace to his tortured spirit.

In *The Idiot*, Dostoevsky is again concerned with the theme of selfishness and vanity, but here he concentrates on the human impulse of taking revenge on others for one's personal failings. All the egocentric characters in this novel strive for power and position, and in the course of these endeavors they inflict suffering upon others. If their selfish desires cannot be satisfied or if their ambitions are thwarted, they often become vindictive. In this connection Lebedev remarks impressively, "There was a certain Malthus posing as a friend of humanity. This friend of humanity, with his ill-founded moral principles and his great vanity, became the devourer of humanity. Hurt the vanity of one of these countless friends of humanity, and he will, from petty vengeance, be ready at once to set fire to the world from all sides." This human propensity to inflict vengeance is discernible in Golyadkin as he tries to persuade himself that "he too, in his turn, could harm others." Since he has no opportunity "to set fire to the world from all sides," or to harm anyone seriously, he celebrates his vengeance in dreams, imagining how he would embarrass or disparage his colleagues in the presence of officials of higher rank. Foma, due to his somewhat superior position in the household of the Krakhotkins, can actually take delight in triumph and power over others. It is quite natural that he chooses his victims from among those who cannot oppose him, or those least likely to wish to do so. The Underground Man, when he suffers defeat at the hands of his schoolmates, takes revenge on Liza, who is unable to defend herself. In *Crime and Punishment*, Raskolnikov also reduces the meek and innocent Sonya to tears because he is infuriated by the collapse of his grand schemes.

Such an attitude often results in suffering for both parties: the one suffers in defeat, the other in the thwarted desire to wreak vengeance. This inevitably incurs the contempt of others and culminates, after the first glow of power and superiority, in a more complete loneliness and loss of esteem. Moreover, the man who seeks revenge often experiences shame at his base motives when he realizes that he is seeking only compensation for his frustration. As a result, he begins to hate the person who supplies the opportunity for vengeance. Dostoevsky gives the perfect formulation of this complex feeling in the statement of old Karamazov, who, when asked why he hated a certain person, replies, "Why? Well, I shall tell you: it is true that he has done me no harm, but I have played on him the most unscrupulously mean trick, and no sooner had I done it, than I began to hate him."

Nastasya Filippovna is one of those figures, in *The Idiot*, who are ready to avenge themselves on others in order to appease their wounded vanity, and who delight in the suffering of their victims. However, she too has no opportunity "to set fire to the world from all sides," and therefore, like the Underground Man, she indulges in petty malice, torturing the defenseless. Her main victim is Ganya Ivolgin because he is also self-centered and thus susceptible to every insult. "Consumed with a longing to be original," to be someone apart from the common people, who are unable to perform great deeds or in any way elevate themselves above others, he decides to marry Totsky's former mistress, Nastasya Filippovna, who, he believes, will receive an impressive dowry from her seducer. With it, Ganya could hope to attract the attention of others and hear them say, "Look, that's Ivolgin, as rich as Croesus!" He desires Nastasya Filippovna's money in order "to become original in the highest degree." "One of the vilest and most hateful things connected with money," Ganya observes, "is that it can buy even talent, and will do so long as the world lasts." "A deep and unchanging consciousness of his lack of talent," Dostoevsky adds with reference to Ganya, "combined with an irresistible longing to persuade himself that he was most original, had rankled in his heart ever since childhood."

The humiliation to which Nastasya Filippovna subjects Ganya, throws further light on his vain character. Degraded in her social standing, Nastasya Filippovna is filled with the desire to avenge herself on her fellow men. Once she perceives her suitor's vanity, she determines to victimize him, and with this in mind, she visits Ganya's family. She expects to be insulted by his mother and sister; this would be one way of wounding Ganya's self-esteem. At her birthday party—attended by personages of dignity and standing—where her betrothal to Ganya is to be announced, she openly accepts money from Rogozhin as advance payment for a night she will spend with him; and as a final blow, she tells Ganya she will not marry him. She explains the motive of her visit to his family: "Dear Ganya, I came and scoffed at you on purpose this afternoon; I came to see for the last time just how much you would swallow. You surprised me, you did, indeed. I had expected a great deal from you, but not that! Could you really marry a woman who accepts pearls like these on the very eve of her marriage? Yet you could come here and expect to be betrothed to me. . . . Is it really true that you would crawl all the way to Vasilyevsky Island for three roubles?"

Suddenly inspired by a further possibility to take revenge, she takes Rogozhin's money and mocks Ganya:

I want to look into your soul for the last time. You have tortured me for the last three months, now it is my turn. Do you see this parcel? It contains a hundred thousand roubles. Now, I am going to throw it into the flames before all these witnesses. As soon as it catches fire, you crawl into the fireplace without your gloves, just with bare hands—but you may turn up your sleeves—and pick the money out of the flames. If you pull it out, it is yours, the hundred thousand roubles are yours! You may burn your fingers a little, of course, but then it's a hundred thousand roubles. Think of it! It won't take you long to snatch it out! And, in the meantime, I shall admire your soul while you crawl into the fireplace for my money!

But Ganya has already borne too much and is not prepared for this last, unexpected humiliation. His vanity will not allow him to stoop so low as to rescue the money with which he could "buy talents with originality" and become a Croesus. "So his self-love is greater than his love for money," decides Nastasya Filippovna and presents it to him; but even now his vanity prevents him from accepting it. Afterwards "he repented a thousand times his having returned the money, although he never ceased to boast of his action. . . . He had time to come to hate the Prince for his sympathy though 'not everyone could have made up his mind' to return the money, but he was tormented by the fact that all his melancholy was nothing but continually suppressed vanity."

Ippolit is another vain character in the novel who would like "to set fire to the world from all sides." He tortures the defenseless General Ivolgin, who is a victim of morbid vanity, sometimes trying to impress others with his feigned heroic deeds, friendships, and connections. As a self-centered person, Ippolit is the cause of much agitation and suffering. His suicide attempt gives rise to alarm and fear among his friends. He is partly responsible for General Ivolgin's death and, with but few exceptions, he tortures friends and family. But he is also capable of unselfish actions: this is evident in the assistance he renders to the family of the destitute physician.

His intention to read his confession to some friends also bears witness to his dual nature: in order not to die completely unnoticed, he wants to be praised for courage in baring his egocentric soul in their presence, but he also has a sincere desire to be one with his audience. "In giving your 'alms' and doing your good deeds, whatever form they take, you give part of yourself and take into yourself a part of others. You mutually absorb one another," Ippolit explains to his listeners. Longing so much for admiration and approbation, Ippolit wishes most of all "to perform his deed" to be able to give "a part of himself" to his friends and to absorb a part of them into himself: "I dreamt that one and all would open their arms, and that they would ask for my forgiveness, and I would ask theirs." He has a suspicion that his confession may provoke mockery and contempt in his listeners. He knows that they are just as vain and lacking in the will to live for the spirit as he himself. They also live for the gratification of their creaturely being and are therefore, like Raskolnikov, dependent upon the "beautiful form" of their "actions, deeds, and words." Ippolit is further convinced that they, like him, have a guilty conscience with regard to their "spiritual world, the higher part of man's being"; yet he craves to subdue his own shame by proclaiming his innermost thoughts and feelings. If their reaction is disdain and scorn, he believes that he will also bear this heroically.

When he finishes his reading, he realizes he has failed, for now there is left within him only a feeling of hatred toward those who have witnessed his defeat and humiliation. Far from crowning him with laurels, they mock him; and he, like Ganya, seeks to console himself with the thought that "not everyone could have made up his mind" to take such a courageous step. Most of all he envies and hates Prince Myshkin, for he senses that the Prince has succeeded where he himself has failed: that the Prince is able to give part of himself and, at the same time, to absorb a part of others. Ippolit's appeal to his audience excites animosity because his listeners unmistakably discern their own vanity in his confession; only Prince Myshkin knows that Ippolit's desire is of a noble nature, that he has longed "to deserve their respect and love."

This alternation between two opposing tendencies is the most sustained feature of Ippolit's character. His natural self, with its vanity, ambition, and feelings of superiority, identifies him with Golyadkin, Foma, and Pralinsky. Like the Underground Man and Raskolnikov, he differs from them by virtue of his intellect.

Other characters in *The Idiot* also give evidence of their dual nature. Nastasya Filippovna illustrates this. Vacillating between the duality of her emotions—selfishness and sacrificial love—she finally succumbs to egocentricity, to which also the Prince falls a victim. She tortures her former lover Totsky by preventing him from marrying Aglaya's sister; she torments Ganya and Rogozhin, but most of all herself by dwelling on her exaggerated guilt and infamy. Pride, vanity, the longing for self-respect, and the desire to free herself from the awareness of her disgrace rage hopelessly within her. As she struggles with herself, she involves others—Prince Myshkin, Rogozhin, and Aglaya—in her distress.

The meeting of Nastasya Filippovna and Aglaya exposes their pride and self-indulgence. They understand that they love themselves above all else, and are determined, if necessary, to sacrifice Prince Myshkin to their ego-gratification. "You could not love him because you are too proud . . . no, not proud, that is an error; because you are too vain . . . no, not quite that either; too self-loving to the point of madness," Aglaya declares to Nastasya Filippovna, giving free rein to her longing for revenge. "The Prince has told me that he hates you," she goes on, knowing full well that this will hurt her rival more than anything else. Nastasya Filippovna, however, does not shrink before this attack: "Do you want me to command him, do you hear, command him, now, at once, to leave you, to remain mine forever? Shall I? Shall I say the word?" she taunts Aglaya in order to demonstrate her own claims on the Prince. Though she may ruin his life, she insists upon her fleeting moment of triumph, she must prove her power to Aglaya.

Aglaya's motives in arranging a meeting of Nastasya Filippovna, the Prince, and herself also spring from vanity. She wishes to see with her own eyes that the Prince loves her more than he does Nastasya Filippovna, and she also desires to witness her rival's suffering. She seeks revenge for the pain and humiliation she has had to endure. Neither woman is capable of compassion for the Prince or Rogozhin. When the Prince hesitates—wondering whether to follow Aglaya, or to remain with Nastasya Filippovna—Aglaya leaves him forever. Her vanity will not tolerate even this brief hesitation. It outweighs her love for Prince Myshkin, whom she deprives of both happiness and peace of mind.

Dostoevsky describes the Prince as his "only beautiful and perfect character." [7] His nature is almost identical with that of Christ. In fact, Dostoevsky in his drafts and notes of 1868 speaks of him as "Prince Christ." [8] In the novel, however, the essence of Myshkin's character, his moral beauty, is not without blemish. In his conversation with Keller, he admits to a series of conflicting thoughts in which base motives mingle with lofty aspirations: "Two thoughts meet. This happens very often. It happens continually to me . . . I reproach myself bitterly for it sometimes. . . . God knows whence they arise and come." There are even traces of Raskolnikov's ambition in Myshkin: the desire to become a Napoleon. "What do *you* think of, when you go mooning about alone? Perhaps you imagine yourself a field-marshal, and think you have conquered Napoleon?" Aglaya inquires. He confesses his secret aspirations: "Upon my word, I think about it, especially when falling asleep. Only it is the Austrians whom I conquer, not Napoleon." The Prince, however, who understands the human heart so well, can only laugh at such ambitions; he, who seldom acts upon a base motive, is always prepared to sacrifice himself for others. Nor can he be overcome by his "double thoughts," for his "spiritual world" always proves to be the stronger.

The persistence with which Dostoevsky treats the theme of vanity and the obvious bias apparent in his gloomy characterizations of Trusotsky and Velchaninov in *The Eternal Husband* are pointed indications of his mounting concern with the problem of man's egocentricity. Although characters in his other novels change—Golyadkin becomes insane; Pralinsky learns a profound though painful lesson; the Underground Man retires into isolation when he recognizes the fundamental baseness of human nature; and Raskolnikov awaits his spiritual regeneration —Velchaninov and Trusotsky remain exactly the same at the end of the novel. They have learned nothing from their errors and are prepared to repeat them. The plot hinges on Velchaninov's guilt feeling toward Trusotsky, with whose wife he had a love affair. This feeling evokes in Velchaninov the awareness of the falsity of his previous life. He begins to question his vanity, love of boasting, and the insults he inflicted on his fellow men

purely for pleasure. He repents this attitude, but knows
well that he will not abandon it in the future. "It is shoot-
ing with blank cartridges! As though I did not know for
certain, that in spite of these fits of tearful remorse and
self-reproach, if the same temptations were to turn up
tomorrow . . . it would inevitably be the same," he admits to himself. When he meets Trusotsky in person, he
hates him: like his egocentric predecessors, he suffers from
the recollection of his own guilt. Since his egoism will
not allow him to recognize this guilt as his own, he attempts to ascribe it to someone else; in his thoughts he
calls Trusotsky "a low fellow," making him responsible
for his, Velchaninov's, personal failings.

His sentiments change abruptly when Liza, his natural daughter, begins to fret for Trusotsky and falls ill in
the house of Velchaninov's friends. While hoping that
his enemy will visit Liza, Velchaninov feels more friendly
toward him and is even prepared to admit his guilt. But
he feels no pity for Trusotsky, and his intention to be
friendly is merely the means to an end: "I want to be
utterly different toward him," he promises Kladviya
Petrovna, "I want to be kind to him. That would be a
good thing on my part. For you know, after all, I have
wronged him!" Once he sees that Trusotsky, although
suffering no less that Velchaninov himself, does not plan
to see Liza, he immediately abandons his good intentions:
"I do not feel in the least guilty toward him now, not
in the least!" His realization of the harm he inflicted
upon Trusotsky years ago fades away at the thought of his
own grievance.

According to the concept of honor upheld by their
society, Trusotsky has every right to challenge Velchaninov to a duel, and this Velchaninov would not have
denied him; but this is not enough. Trusotsky's enemy is
a fearless man, to whom a duel would cause little worry
or distress; but Trusotsky wants to see him suffer. To this
end, he is prepared to employ any means, including the
fatal neglect of Liza. "He will take his revenge on me
through Liza," Velchaninov fears, "he is using Liza to

torment me, that is clear!" "How could that monster be so cruel to a child whom he had loved so much? Is it credible?" he asks himself. "But every time he thinks of it, he makes haste to dismiss that question, brushes it aside, as it were, since there is something awful in it, something he cannot bear and cannot solve." He shudders to think of the intensity of such an ego-drive turned loose; that in order to avenge himself man can lose every trace of pity for others; that injured self-love can spur him so far that, for the sheer delight of revenge, he is ready to sacrifice the life of an innocent human being. The little girl dies as a result of the selfishness of these two men: Velchaninov, through whose guilt she was born; and Trusotsky, who has more concern for his humiliation than for the innocent child.

The theme of vanity and suffering also finds expression in the short story "The Gentle Maiden." It is a story of a man who is compelled to retire from the service because of his cowardly failure to defend the honor of his regiment when called upon to do so. After his resignation, he revels in his own disgrace like Nastasya Filippovna in *The Idiot*. Too proud to accept private employment, he decides to indulge in self-humiliation: "Shame upon shame, ignominy upon ignominy, failure upon failure, and the worse the better, that is what I choose for my position." A small legacy then enables him to make a beginning in business. He becomes a pawnbroker intentionally to flaunt his low position before the society to which he had previously belonged. Now he can dwell on his degradation by constantly reminding himself that his present occupation is dishonorable and disgraceful for a Russian nobleman and a former officer. He also has ample opportunity to gloat over the misery of the people who come to his establishment in financial distress. In this occupation, his embitterment and hatred are increasingly intensified. Finally he marries a poor but proud young girl who comes to his shop to pawn her last belongings. He cherishes the hope that in her gratitude she will give him the love and respect which his wounded pride so much desires. His plan is to remain "proud and stern, as one who does not need any moral consolation and suffers in silence." He wants her to understand his character without his help: "In time she will see that this is magnanimity on my part, and as soon as she sees my true nature, she will value me twofold, and fall on her knees with her hands folded in prayer." He loves and admires her profoundly, but does not divulge his true feelings: with this apparent callousness he tries to gain her respect and affection. The young woman at first cannot understand him, later her genuine feeling of love for him dies, and they live in silence and mutual isolation.

When, after his wife's suicide, the pawnbroker reviews his married life, he tries to determine the cause of their tragedy. "It was her fault, her fault alone," he says to himself, thinking that she, in her concern only for herself, could "forget him," could simply abandon him in his grief without having extended a helping hand. Conscious only of her own pain and humiliation, she was no longer capable of love for her tortured husband, but rather than deceive him, committed suicide, plunging from a window with the very icon that she had pawned in his shop clasped in her hands. When the pawnbroker considers the tragedy from her point of view, he admits his guilt, because in striving for self-assertion he had driven her to rebellion and had crushed her natural love for him. For the sheer pleasure of wounding her pride, he had pointed out that she owed him her sustenance, and further insulted her by suddenly appearing at her meeting with the officer who was responsible for his resignation from the regiment. He even made this more obvious by giving the officer the opportunity to insult him in her presence, and finally added to her distress by pretending to sleep while she held the pistol at his head, to show her that he was still in control of the situation. In their mutual silence and self-indulgence, Dostoevsky discloses the roots of their isolation. They share equal guilt for the ensuing tragedy.

In "The Dream of a Ridiculous Man," Dostoevsky's familiar concern with psychological delineation of character is noticeably lacking. Here, the writer is more interested in egocentricity as an idea rather than as a trait in the personality of his hero. The Ridiculous Man is not an individual, but man in general. He seeks to assert his personality in order to gratify his ego; he abandons this idea when he sees he cannot win the respect of his fellow men, who refuse to take him seriously. He is overcome by apathy, that state which Golyadkin instinctively feared, which took possession of Raskolnikov temporarily, and which drove Svidrigaylov and Stravrogin to suicide. Like that of his predecessors, the Ridiculous Man's dejection springs from his inability to find any meaning in existence. Since nothing interests him, he becomes indifferent to all that exists. "The conviction came upon me," he reflects, "that *nothing in the world mattered*. . . . I suddenly felt that it was *all the same* to me whether the world existed or whether there had never been anything at all." He is fully aware that his indifference and weariness of life are traceable to shame at being unable to assert himself, and at appearing ridiculous: "Everybody always laughed at me, but none of them knew or guessed that if there were one man on earth who knew better than anybody else that I was ridiculous, it was myself, and what I resented most of all was that they did not know it." This notwithstanding, he refuses to confess to them that he is ridiculous, because in this way he would admit his inferiority: "I was so proud that nothing would have induced me to tell it to anyone . . . and if I allowed myself to own to anyone that I was ridiculous, I believe that I should have blown out my brains the same evening." So long as he suffers because of the low opinion others have of him, he does have a connection with their world, even if only through his feeling of shame and inferiority. This sensation is his last remaining link with other people and with human society. Lacking, however, a belief in absolute values, he would sever himself completely from their world if he abandoned his vanity by an open confession to others of his oddity and stupidity.

Everyday life does not interest the Ridiculous Man; nor does he have a belief in immortality and God. "If I am going to kill myself in two hours," he reflects, "what have I to do with the whole world?" His loneliness and disbelief in personal immortality make the earthly world seem unreal to him. Only his own self has any actual significance for him. His isolation is so enveloping that the whole universe appears only in relation to himself: "It seems to me that life and the world somehow depend on me now. I may almost say that the world now seems created for me alone. . . . Nothing will exist for anyone when I am gone and my consciousness is extinguished; the whole world and all these people are only I myself."

To put an end to his depression, he resolves to commit suicide, but falls asleep in the midst of these reflections. In a dream he perceives a revelation of truth, and becomes conscious of man's egocentricity as the origin of suffering. Self-indulgence, the fear of ridicule, man's isolation, and the necessity to believe in a personal immortality are shown in *The Dream* to be intimately related.

Whereas in Dostoevsky's earlier works, the complex manifestations of egocentricity are emphasized, in "The Dream of a Ridiculous Man" the writer penetrates still further and discovers that the origin of human egoism and suffering is in man's reason. Once feeling is forsaken for reason, the result is discord and isolation, and there begins the "struggle for separation, for individuality, for mine and thine." When knowledge is valued above feeling, mankind "learns to lie, grows fond of it, comes to know shame, and elevates shame to virtue." Dostoevsky's description of the Golden Age is that of the earth before the Fall. On the dream-planet of the Ridiculous Man, sin is unknown, mutual love is instinctive, life is peaceful, and death is but a gentle falling asleep. Man has no creed; instead he possesses a sense of unity with the entire universe. The Ridiculous Man is an intruder who corrupts this sinless society. Following the allegory of the Fall in the Old Testament, Dostoevsky shows how evil is activated on the imaginary planet through initial consciousness of its existence. This point of view was later expressed by Martin Buber: "The opposition of good and evil, which have been always latent in the created world, forces its way into actual reality through man's awareness of this opposition: from this moment on it becomes existent." [9]

Dostoevsky describes civilization as a product of the activity of reason, as a condition which gives rise to vanity, revenge, ambition, sensuality, and delight in evil. Since reason can corrupt human nature, Dostoevsky considers it as a potential evil. As such, it can become a stumbling block in man's striving for moral and spiritual self-betterment. Even at the age of eighteen, Dostoevsky refused to accept reason as the source of knowledge.

> Nature, the soul, love, and God, one recognizes through the heart, and not through reason. If we were spirits, we could dwell in that region of ideas over which our souls hover, seeking the solution. But we are earthbound beings, and can only guess at the Idea—not grasp it by all sides at once. The guide for our intellect through the temporary illusion into the innermost center of the soul is called *Reason*. Now, Reason is a material capacity, while the soul or spirit lives on the thoughts which are whispered by the heart. Thoughts are born in the soul. Reason is a tool, a machine, which is driven by the spiritual flame."[10]

Reason, as an intermediary between man's spiritual and animal nature, is a positive human quality. It is necessary in order to convey the revelations of man's spiritual being to his physical self. But reason is the source of man's dual nature for it gives man the freedom of choice between gratification of earthly impulses and spiritual endeavor. With the loss of his ability to reason, neither this choice nor suffering would fall to his lot; he would be relieved of his duality and sin. Paradise on earth—the dream of the Ridiculous Man—would be immediately established.

Dostoevsky depicts the tragic consequences which arise when man neglects the voice of conscience and bases his actions entirely upon logic and intelligence, which are inadequate as guides for human behavior in Dostoevsky's eyes. The moral disintegration of the inhabitants of the dream-planet begins when reason is substituted for feeling as the moral foundation in life, for this distorts the heart and mind. "Knowledge is higher than feeling," they now argue, "the consciousness of life is higher than life itself. Science will give us reason, wisdom will reveal the laws; and the knowledge of the laws of happiness is higher than happiness itself." [11] As a result of this new attitude, everyone, Dostoevsky says, "has begun to love himself more than anyone else. . . . All have become so jealous of their own personality that they do their utmost to curtail or destroy it in others, and have made this the chief purpose of their lives. Slavery has appeared, even voluntary slavery; the weak have eagerly submitted to the strong, on condition that the latter aid them to subdue the still weaker."

Dostoevsky's youthful conviction, that in order to live a righteous life man must first of all rely on intuition and obey the voice of conscience, remained his lifelong belief. It reappears often in his works in such characters as Sonya Marmeladov, Prince Myshkin, Sofya Andreevna Dolgoruky, Alyosha Karamazov, and Father Zosima, whose actions are primarily instinctive. The tragedy of Dostoevsky's intellectual heroes originates in their failure to acknowledge the value of the intuitive affirmation and acceptance of life that are exemplified, for example, by Sonya Marmeladov. Instead, they give priority to the rational over the irrational, and are unable to recognize "nature, the soul, love, and God . . . through the heart." [12] This failure results in spiritual disintegration. The evil which underlies man's everlasting contradictions, if he has only reason upon which to depend, is thus purely rational in origin.

In the novels of Dostoevsky, the theme of duality and ambition is central to his ethical and moral speculations. In exposing the various aspects of this problem, he shows isolation as the logical consequence of man's drive to gratify his natural self. This isolation is developed parallel to the theme of suffering in almost all his works.

Golyadkin, Prokharchin, the Underground Man, Svidrigaylov, Stavrogin, the pawnbroker in "The Gentle
Maiden," and the Ridiculous Man are all self-centered
people who at the same time display the fatal results of
isolation. Raskolnikov, for example, prior to his crime,
lives in self-imposed seclusion. Like the Ridiculous Man,
he is engrossed in himself to the exclusion of all others.
After the crime, his isolation is intensified. Separated
from everybody, with his whole life "lying at the bottom
of some fathomless chasm, deep, deep down, where he
could just discern dimly his old thoughts, problems, subjects, impressions," he feels like one condemned to death.
He, too, experiences an urge to communicate his thoughts
to others, but he resists this desire. He hates himself because in spite of his unbearable isolation he still clings to
a life which has lost all meaning for him. His greatest
torment is the realization that he will be *alone* for the
rest of his life.[13]

Similarly, Svidrigaylov in *Crime and Punishment* commits suicide because he also cannot bear to face the loneliness of his life. A sense of inner isolation prompts the
suicide of both Smerdyakov in *The Brothers Karamazov*
and Ippolit in *The Idiot*. They all lead egocentric and
secluded lives, remaining selfish even in the hour of their
death: they do not die for others, but for themselves.

Stavrogin in *The Possessed* is an example of the man
who feels the barrier separating him from his fellow men
so strongly that his life appears to him devoid of all meaning or purpose. His spiritual impasse is brought about
both by the collapse of the self-centered rationalistic basis
of his existence and by his insurmountable isolation. He
fails to find the truth and faith for which he longs, and is
driven to suicide in the manner of Svidrigaylov. In
Stavrogin's case, Dostoevsky stresses—as in Raskolnikov's
delirious dream of microcosmic creatures endowed with
reason and will—that the individual is fated to perish
spiritually if his life is guided entirely by reason and
dialectic.

The full realization of the tragic consequences of man's

isolation receives artistic expression in the person of the pawnbroker in "The Gentle Maiden," who is able to discern the reasons for his distress only upon his wife's death: "Stagnation! Oh, Nature! Men are alone on earth—that is the misfortune! 'Is there a living man in the field?' cries the Russian hero. I cry the same, though not a hero, and no one answers my cry. . . . Everything is dead, and everywhere there are the dead. Only men and silence round them—this is the earth!" Man is alone, "he is trapped in his singleness, in his egoistic self-consciousness. Only through merging of the self in the totality, in brotherhood, will man break out of the circle of his loneliness." [14] It is only after his wife's death that the pawnbroker understands that she fell victim to their mutual silence and isolation, their egocentricity and sole concern with their individual problems.

Closely linked with Dostoevsky's artistic analysis of the consequences of isolation is the theme of shame. Isolation is accompanied by shame, though it does not appear certain which of these two phenomena is primary. The novelist shows them as closely related to each other, and interdependent. The Ridiculous Man fears to appear ludicrous; this feeling removes him further from his fellows. At the same time it intensifies his conviction of the futility of life and deprives him of belief in immortality. To fill this void, he substitutes preoccupation with his own personality. His feeling of shame is not born from a desire to feel himself above others, but rather from a desperate wish not to feel lower. When people ridicule him, he is afraid they place him lower than themselves. This fear hurts the Ridiculous Man's self-esteem most painfully. Essentially indifferent to everybody and everything, he is disturbed only by the possibility of being considered as an inferior.

Shame, or the fear of appearing ridiculous, is the greatest tragedy of several of Dostoevsky's characters. This feeling—the inability to overcome shame—leads to the impasse of Stavrogin and destroys his last hope for life. He does his utmost to manifest his fearlessness and indifference to human laws and opinions, but there is still inherent in him the fear of ridicule. In striving to give life some solidity and meaning, as we learn from the suppressed chapter in *The Possessed*, he goes to Tikhon with a confession which he desires to be made public. He wants to make his previous crimes known to be able to repent and be forgiven, and thus to re-establish his bond with others, to become one with them. Tikhon, however, anticipates that Stavrogin will not be able to overcome his fear of shame and knows beforehand that the latter will never publish the manuscript. Stavrogin, too, realizes that he will not endure the mockery of his townsmen, especially that of Liza. He even consents to the murder of his wife in order to maintain the secrecy of his crimes. Liza feels that Stavrogin's conscience is ominously burdened: "I ought to confess that ever since those days in Switzerland I have had a strong feeling that you have something awful, loathsome, some bloodshed on your conscience . . . and yet something that would make you look ridiculous. Beware of telling me: if it is true, I shall laugh you to scorn. I shall laugh at you for the rest of your life." [15]

Stavrogin's new crime, perpetrated to escape appearing ridiculous in Liza's eyes, separates them from each other; and having lost his last hope of the possibility of regeneration through love, of a new life in harmony with others, Stavrogin commits suicide. The Ridiculous Man would probably have ended his life in the same way, if his dream had not saved him.

Dostoevsky considers the emotion of shame to be a factor which distorts man's nature and which may even lead to his corruption. Dostoevsky's egocentric characters, impelled by burning shame, become absorbed in their own selves to the exclusion of everything else. This absorption, in turn, heightens their isolation, and this results in still greater depression. And so the process continues until finally they are convinced of the futility of life.

Dostoevsky develops this theme in *Notes from the*

Underground. The Underground Man suffers from a consuming shame. He himself admits that he feels two diametrically opposed elements within him which torture him and drive him to convulsions. In his humiliation he vows never to allow "these elements of the most opposite order conceivable" to manifest themselves outwardly. He tries to suppress them, but this same suppression turns against him. In a similar way, Raskolnikov is ashamed of his surrender to the "laws of nature," to his evil instincts. When he sees that he has failed to gratify his "flesh and lust," he "falls ill from injured pride." In *The Eternal Husband*, Trusotsky, in order to escape humiliation and regain his social status, decides to avenge himself on Velchaninov by neglecting the dying Liza, regardless of how much personal grief it may cause him. The grievous consequences of shame are also exposed in "The Gentle Maiden" where the pawnbroker tells his wife that the fear of appearing ridiculous ruined his military career and forced him to take up his despicable occupation.

The theme of shame as the cause of suffering is presented most forcefully in *The Brothers Karamazov*. Fyodor Pavlovich Karamazov becomes an avaricious libertine, a cruel husband, and an indifferent father because of this emotion which originates in his feeling of worthlessness. Father Zosima, who comprehends the true source of Fyodor Pavlovich's distorted nature, advises him, "And, above all, do not be ashamed of yourself, for that is the root of all." Old Karamazov's reply reveals with even greater urgency the cause of his corruption:

> You pierced me to the heart with that remark, and saw right through me. Indeed, it always seems to me when I meet people that I am the lowest of all, and that they take me for a fool. So I say: "Let me really play the fool. I am not afraid of your opinion, for you are, everyone of you, worse than I am!" That is why I am a fool. It is from shame, Reverend Father, from shame; it is simply self-consciousness which makes me evil. If I had only been sure that everyone would accept me as a most amiable and wise man, oh, Lord, what a good man I should have been then!

To hide his weaknesses, he is forced to lie to himself and to others. Father Zosima, aware of this propensity in Fyodor Pavlovich's character, further counsels him, "Above all, do not lie to yourself. The man who lies to himself and listens to his own lies comes to such a pass that he cannot distinguish the truth within himself or around him . . . and so ceases to love; and in order to occupy and distract himself without love, he gives way to passions and coarse pleasures, sinking to bestiality in his vice, all from continual lying to other men and to himself."

Fyodor Pavlovich's dissolute life results in the suffering and death of both his wives, and also brings misfortune upon his children. Dmitry, like his father, becomes an idle profligate, a thief and almost a murderer. Ivan, a moral accomplice in his father's murder, is tormented by guilt feelings. He is inconsolable after discovering that his father's fear of ridicule is latent within him, and is shaken when Smerdyakov, who knows the full extent of Ivan's covert vanity, tells him that he is "like Fyodor Pavlovich, more like him than any of his other children." Ivan cannot endure the thought that he, the man who refused to acknowledge any power beyond his control and who despises men as slaves, should be ashamed of himself and, in cowardly fashion, attempt to conceal from others his abominable complicity in his father's murder. This reaffirms his determination to report himself to the authorities. He will show that he is not ashamed to come before them; he will display his contempt for their judgment and for their revulsion. He will go before them and say, "I killed him! Why do you writhe in horror? I despise your opinion, I despise your horror!" In his torment he believes he hears his alter ego, the devil, say to him, "You will go because of your pride. You will stand up and say, 'It was I who killed him. . . . I despise your opinion!' . . . but secretly you are longing for their praise: 'He is a criminal, a murderer, but what a generous soul! He wanted to save his brother and confessed!'" Later Ivan admits that his courage and contempt for others are nothing but lies, just as it was with Fyodor Pavlovich. The discovery that it is vanity which he attempts to cover with a mask of generosity proves more than he can endure. "I do not want the rabble to praise me! . . . I swear I don't!" he assures Alyosha. In a fit of weakness, he sinks to the level of Golyadkin, wishing that the apparition with its debased thoughts were really a devil, and not he, Ivan, himself. "I would be awfully glad to think that it was really *he* and not I," he confesses to his younger brother.

In psychological terms, this hallucination is an example of how man's spiritual breakdown, on the one hand, leads to neurosis, and on the other, gives us a deeper insight into the metaphysical facets of duality. It is very clear from a letter to Dr. A. F. Blagonravov that Dostoevsky himself did not consider Ivan's devil to be the devil of the Bible or of legend:

> Because of the chapter in *The Karamazovs* (the one about Ivan's hallucination) with which you, as a physician, are so pleased, attempts have been made to stamp me as a reactionary and fanatic, who has written to the point of seeing devils. In their naiveté, they imagine that everybody will shout, "What? Dostoevsky has begun to write about devils now, has he? How dull and boring he is!" . . . I am grateful to you, as an expert in the matter, for your opinion concerning the believable portrayal of Ivan's mental illness. . . . You will, I have no doubt, agree that this man (Ivan Karamazov), in the given circumstances, could have no other hallucination than this one.[16]

All that Ivan considers evil in his nature—a desire to evade the responsibility for his suppressed vanity and cowardly actions, a wish to avoid knowledge of them in the disgraceful manner of Golyadkin, a refusal to accept God's creation and man's suffering—is epitomized by the devil. In him, Ivan recognizes with disgust his own servile soul, that aspect of his nature which longs for evil deeds, but loathes the thought of performing them. He who craved to become a Titan for whom "all things are lawful," is no more than a vain "servile lackey," a "scoundrel," a "sponger with good taste."

All of Dostoevsky's egocentric characters are slaves to their creaturely being, tortured by their fear of shame and vanity, their desire for superiority and power, and their reason devoid of intuitive support. In these manifestations of man's natural self, Dostoevsky sees the fundamental reality of a human being. In a vivid portrayal of the yawning gap between man's spiritual capacities and his creaturely self, the novelist heralds the principal theme of his writings: in order to do justice to the divine image within himself, man must conquer his vanity and fear of appearing ridiculous; he must be ready to accept self-knowledge unflinchingly, for the espousal of truth is the first and foremost prerequisite for spiritual perfection.

IN SEEKING TO REVEAL the tragedy of man as a dual being, Dostoevsky portrays the abnormal states of the psyche, all phenomena of which he considers manifestations of higher metaphysical realities. And an understanding of Dostoevsky's metaphysics of evil is necessary for one to discern the primal tragedy, which comes to the fore in his more mature works, particularly *The Brothers Karamazov*, where evil is expressed both in metaphysical and psychological terms. "The Legend of the Grand Inquisitor," an expression of Ivan Karamazov's rebellion against God, stands in close connection with Dostoevsky's earlier writings, for it discloses more of the concept of duality which underlies the works previously examined. It reflects Dostoevsky's lifelong study of man as a "mixture of the heavenly and the earthly," [1] the problem which tormented his mind even when he was at the Military Engineers' Academy.

After the portrayal of man with inherent egocentricity, vanity, and other facets of his creaturely being, Dostoevsky arranges a trial, as it were, at which the Grand Inquisitor points out to Christ that God created man as the least perfect of all creatures. He burdened man with an animal being and so condemned him to continual suffering. The Grand Inquisitor appears as the defense counsel for man, the victim of God, Who has endowed him with a dual nature which man is too weak to bear with dignity. He elaborates his defense by showing that in most cases man either becomes a prey to his creaturely being or revolts against God. In neither of these instances does man strive for spiritual and moral perfection as should a creature made in the divine image. In the name of mankind, the Grand Inquisitor brings against Christ three charges. First of all, he states, man has earthly needs and a natural impulse to satisfy them. Man's freedom of spirit and the exercise of his will are impeded by these natural needs. How is it possible, the Grand Inquisitor asks, to reproach man with his efforts to maintain natural existence, an existence which requires, first and foremost, that his hunger be allayed? He rebukes Christ that He did not take from men the worry over their daily bread. As freedom of spirit can scarcely be reconciled with the natural needs of human beings, they abandon this freedom and say, "Make us your slaves, but feed us." The Grand Inquisitor says to Christ, "They themselves will understand at last that freedom and bread, enough for all, are inconceivable together, for never, never will they be able to share among themselves." There are but few people who have enough strength to neglect their animal being for the sake of living for the spirit. "And, if for the sake of the bread of Heaven, thousands will follow Thee, what is to become of the millions and tens of thousands of millions of creatures who have not the strength to forgo the earthly bread for the sake of the heavenly?" the Grand Inquisitor proceeds. He believes that, had Christ freed men from the anxiety associated with their earthly needs, He would have lifted the burden of suffering which arises from the duality of human nature. Their question as to whom they should worship would then have been answered. Man, relieved of this anxiety, would no longer doubt his Creator, for "man seeks to worship what is established beyond any dispute."

Man as a spiritual being, the Grand Inquisitor continues, needs worship as an expression of belief in immortality; but even if he succeeds in worshipping something "established beyond any dispute," he cannot be happy so long as he is devoid of the feeling of unity with humanity. This feeling of isolation deprives him of contentment with life. "The craving for *community* of worship is the chief misery of every man individually and of all humanity from the beginning of time," the Grand Inquisitor insists. Man's worry about his natural existence, however, forces him to struggle against his fellow men. Man is turned against man because they stand in a relationship similar to that of one animal toward another, each trying to seize the other's food. The animal is not disturbed by the question of whether or not this lies in the nature of universal laws, but man suffers under the law of the jungle, for it conflicts with his conscience. Had Christ freed men from the worry about their daily bread, He would also have freed them from this primitive state, and consequently from a stricken conscience: "And behold, instead of providing a firm foundation for setting the conscience of man at rest forever, Thou didst choose all that is exceptional, vague and enigmatic; Thou didst choose what was utterly beyond the strength of man, acting as if Thou didst not love him at all." The Grand Inquisitor considers that Christ demanded too much of man, and that His love for humanity was too uncompromising; it was directed toward man as he should be, and not as he is.

The second reproach of the Grand Inquisitor is that Christ withheld "miracle, mystery, and authority." Christ did not cast Himself down the mountain, nor did He descend from the cross. He submitted His body to the natural laws, for He did not want "to enslave man by a miracle." Man, however, a rebel by nature, will try to conquer these natural laws and rise above them, and a significant part of the tragedy of Dostoevsky's heroes lies in this struggle, for such attempts lead only to inevitable failure and spiritual pain. Raskolnikov strove to become a superman, stronger than that nature which condemned him to cling to his "flesh and lust." The Underground Man tried to run against "the wall of the laws of nature," although he knew full well the utter futility of his endeavor. Kirillov wanted, through suicide, to initiate the transformation of man into superman; and Ivan Karamazov, too, thought that he could disregard the laws of nature. All these attempts resulted only in suffering.

The Grand Inquisitor says to Christ, "Thou didst hope that man, following Thee, could cling to God and not ask for a miracle." Had Christ left the possibility of a miracle—a gap in the wall of nature—men would have followed Him, for "men are slaves, of course, though created rebels." Since the causal laws of nature exclude the miracle, man's faith grows weaker. Raskolnikov, dissatisfied with the social structure of the community—which is for him the consequence of causal laws—rages against God's creation and feels himself justified in attempting to improve it. The Underground Man, too, driven to desperation, tries to smash "the wall of the laws of nature." He cannot, in his state, be reconciled with God's creation or believe in Christ's love for man. Kirillov, who admired Christ's martyrdom, does not recognize the causal laws as ordained by God. He intends to free himself from subservience to them, and thus to point the way for humanity through his suicide. In a determination to destroy God, he aims at making the world happy.

Dostoevsky considers the causal laws of nature to be an apparent antithesis to the spiritual aspect of God's creation. "The highest heavenly world," as Father Zosima terms it, or "the higher noble spirituality," [2] in Dostoevsky's words, is in utter contradiction with the earthly laws to which all men are subjected, irrespective of their denial of God's existence. Therefore, the Grand Inquisitor tells Christ that while these causal laws prevail, a weak man believes his faith in God and his striving to "the higher spiritual world" to be futile. The Grand Inquisitor's fears are justified in the case of Raskolnikov, the Underground Man, and Smerdyakov, who are unable to accept the world—in which the scoundrel prospers and the righteous man perishes—as a creation of a kind and merciful God. From this viewpoint, the Grand Inquisitor maintains that a miracle or "a gap in the wall of the laws of nature" can give man a belief in God and immortality, a belief which is essential for his peace of mind. If Christ had left for man a belief in the possibility of a miracle, he would have acquired his faith undisturbed by doubt, he would have attained peace and happiness. The immutability of the causal laws not only reduces him to "the last and the least of creatures," but is also the reason that in the whole creation of God "the law of spiritual nature is . . . violated." The Grand Inquisitor raises this violation as his second charge against Christ. Duality in the structure of the world makes man a wretched slave of the relentless laws of nature, a plaything in the hands of some all-powerful force. Out of compassion for man, the Grand Inquisitor censures Christ for His failure to abolish through a miracle this painful duality.

As in the argument presented by Glaucon and Adeimantus in Plato's *Republic*,[3] Dostoevsky's rebellious characters such as Raskolnikov, the Underground Man, and even Ivan Karamazov, are ready to worship and believe in God if they can be sure of a reward. The valet Smerdyakov is also prepared to revere God if he is to be rewarded for his faith. He arrives at the conclusion that, since he cannot bid his faith to move a mountain, Heaven will not esteem highly his religious feeling, "for since the mountain had not moved at my word, they cannot think very much of my faith in Heaven, and there cannot be a great reward awaiting me in the world to come. So why should I let them flay me alive as well, and to no good purpose?" For Smerdyakov, thus, there is no virtue without a reward. Even old Karamazov is aroused at such an interpretation of the Christian faith. Raskolnikov has a similar view of Christianity. He believes Sonya actually out of her mind to worship God without a reward. He witnesses the ruin of her family and cannot understand that, regardless of this, she still entrusts herself to a God Who can permit such an injustice as her terrible and shameful position in the community. Raskolnikov asks himself, when he thinks of Sonya, the tragedy of her future and that of her family, "What is she waiting for? A miracle?" He believes she endures her hard life only in the expectation of a miracle, a reward from God for her firm religious faith.

On the death of Father Zosima, his followers also expect a miracle as recompense for his life of purity. When none takes place and his body begins to decompose in accordance with the laws of nature, even Alyosha is shaken and, through his sorrow, driven almost to sin. The followers have already forgotten Father Zosima's words on the pure act of faith: "Children, seek no miracles. Miracles will kill faith." The Underground Man, too, denounces virtue without reward, and the noble-minded Ivan Karamazov's menial ego says to him, "Only those who have no conscience gain, for how can they be tortured by conscience when they have none? But decent people who have conscience and honor suffer for it." In despair, Ivan can only reply, "How could my soul beget such a creature as you?" whereupon the devil explains to him that this creature is the author of "The Legend of the Grand Inquisitor," and that the latter is the advocate for all such weaklings. The Grand Inquisitor is prepared to give man a longed-for miracle, since "man seeks not so much God as the miraculous," whereas Christ, craving "faith given freely," refused "to enslave men by a miracle."

The pawnbroker in "The Gentle Maiden" desires his wife's love "given freely," not based on compulsion. In this he resembles Christ in "The Legend of the Grand Inquisitor." The pawnbroker's wife, however, is too weak to measure up to such demands; in order to gain her confidence and love, her husband would have had to give her proof of his love for her, just as in "The Legend" Christ would have had to come down from the cross in order to win the love and faith of man. When the pawnbroker realizes that he was wrong in his expectations, he also grasps his wife's weakness. He, too, had rated her too highly, whereas she was only "a slave, even though rebellious by nature." Similarly, she revolted against her husband because he was a coward and a weakling. He should have shown her his power, or bribed her with love and compassion. Virtue without a reward did not exist for her any more than it existed for Golyadkin, Raskolnikov, and Ivan Karamazov.

The third reproach of the Grand Inquisitor is that Christ rejected the sword of Caesar and bequeathed to man a freedom in his decisions and actions, a freedom which will lead him to ruin. The Grand Inquisitor bitterly attacks Christ for His love, which has become a burden rather than a blessing for humanity: He has given men freedom of conscience for which they are too weak. He therefore says to Christ, "Hadst Thou accepted that last counsel of the mighty spirit, Thou wouldst have accomplished all that man seeks on earth, that is, Thou wouldst have given him someone to worship, someone to entrust his conscience to, and some means of unifying all into one unanimous and harmonious ant-heap."

The thought that man tries to shun all responsibility for the sins and actions which weigh heavily on his conscience was expressed by Dostoevsky for the first time in *The Double*. Golyadkin, when he can no longer manage his double, is willing to sacrifice his personal freedom for peace of mind. When he fails to achieve power and authority over others, he attempts to avoid self-reproaches by disclaiming the responsibility for his actions: "I look upon you, my benefactor and superior, as a father, and entrust my fate to you, and I will not say anything against your decisions; I put myself in your hands, and retire from the affair." He seeks someone to whom he can transfer the heavy burden of his conscience. In his anguish, he visualizes some magician who comes to him saying, "Give a finger from your right hand, Golyadkin, and we shall call it quits; the other Golyadkin will no longer exist, and you will be happy, only you will not have your finger." "Yes, I would sacrifice my finger," Golyadkin admits, "I certainly would!"

Men long to obey the one who can shoulder this encumbrance for them. "They will submit to us gladly and cheerfully," the Grand Inquisitor observes, "and they will be glad to believe our decisions, for it will save them from the great anxiety and terrible agony they endure at present in making a free decision for themselves." He believes that since man is continually torn between his spiritual and creaturely being, a freedom to govern his own decisions can only result in suffering. As man is weak and afraid of suffering, he will always seek someone whom he can make responsible for his actions.

Man's fear of assuming responsibility for his deeds prompts the Grand Inquisitor to relieve man of his duality by denying him conscience, "the greatest anxiety and terrible agony in making a free decision for himself." Once man is unburdened of this "terrible gift that has brought him so much suffering," he will rejoice and be happy. Christ's way of life has proven to be only for "the strong and elect," those who can cope with their freedom of conscience. Troubled by the thought of the weak ones, the Grand Inquisitor asks, "Are they to blame because they could not endure what the strong have endured? . . . Canst Thou have come only to the elect and for the elect?" In their freedom of conscience, given to men by Christ, they are tormented by their sins, and, like Golyadkin, they would like to appeal to "a bene-factor and superior," as if to a father who would free them from conscience and, by so doing, allow them to sin again. "Oh, we shall even allow them to sin; they are weak and helpless, and they will love us like children be-cause we allow them to sin. We shall tell them that every sin will be expiated, if it is done with our permis-sion," the Grand Inquisitor promises Christ. If there is someone to accept responsibility for man's sin, his con-science will no longer suffer. If laws allow man to succumb to sins, he must have no feeling of guilt.

The Grand Inquisitor warns Christ that there are few elect people who can bear responsibility alone. "And be-sides," he proceeds, "how many of those elect, those mighty ones who could have become elect, have grown weary waiting for Thee, and have transferred and will transfer the power of their spirit and the ardor of their heart to the other camp, and end by raising their free

banner against Thee." Raskolnikov has the strength
to shoulder the responsibility for his murder and its consequences. However, even though filled with genuine
Christian compassion and sympathy for the suffering
and oppressed, he directs his strength against Christ for
the sake of his "flesh and lust." A further revolt against
Christ is Raskolnikov's wish to change Sonya's Christian
state of mind—all-enduring and sacrificial—into hatred
toward her tormentors. The Grand Inquisitor refers to
this attitude of Raskolnikov's in speaking of those who
could have become the elect, but turned their free banner
against Christ.

Svidrigaylov, Kirillov, Stavrogin, Versilov, and Ivan
Karamazov also could have become elect, but they end in
laying hands either on themselves or on others, raising
in this way their free banner against Christ. With the
excepton of Kirillov, they are all slaves to the "coarse
veil" [4] of earth and the causal laws of nature against
which they clamor so loudly. Even Kirillov, in the last
minutes before suicide, is transformed from a man-god
into a weakling through his subjection to the "earthly veil
of matter."

In his logically developed argument the Grand Inquisitor has, however, missed one important possibility.
He does not take into consideration the fact that these
same mutineers, if given the opportunity, can find their
way back to Christ. Raskolnikov, who is prepared to suffer
in atonement for his crime, finally becomes enlightened
and, having won the battle against his base instincts, is
now ready to raise the banner for Christ. As will be
shown later, Dostoevsky implies that such conflicts in
the human mind are necessary to determine the meaning
of earthly life. The conflict between Raskolnikov's denial
and Sonya's acceptance of divine justice is of this nature.
But the Grand Inquisitor, even though he understands
the purpose of these antitheses, refuses to accept them.
This appears to be the reason that he can see only the
dark side of the rebel's actions: his mutiny against God
and Christ.

From the Grand Inquisitor's three charges against

Christ, man's spiritual suffering is shown to have its roots in his freedom of conscience, and the only way of relieving man from the mental pain caused by his duality is to deny him this freedom, the Grand Inquisitor suggests, since freedom and happiness are for him incompatible. In freedom, man is a slave and a rebel at the same time; yet if he is deprived of freedom, he will remain only a slave, and the pain arising from his duality will be eliminated. Had the Grand Inquisitor succeeded in freeing man from his burden of conscience, he would have removed the main source of man's mental anguish and enabled those "millions of men," who are his chief concern, to live a quiet and peaceful life, without suffering, without the pricks of conscience, and without a struggle for existence. This condition can be achieved only by depriving man of his divine image and of his chance to live for the spirit.

"The roots of man's thoughts and feelings are not here, but in other worlds," insists Father Zosima. In taking from man freedom of conscience, the Grand Inquisitor would have also lost for him a connection with "other worlds." As Father Zosima maintains, "the spiritual world, the higher part of man's being, would then be rejected altogether and banished." This possibility does not perturb the Grand Inquisitor because he cannot believe in man's divine origin, as he does not believe in God. Alyosha Karamazov recognizes this clearly when he replies to Ivan, "Your Inquisitor does not believe in God, that's his whole secret!" But even the Grand Inquisitor himself fears that an animal existence will never suffice for man, since he admits, "The secret of man's being is not only to live, but to have something to live for. Without a steadfast faith in the object of life, man would not consent to go on living, but would rather destroy himself than remain on earth, though he had bread in abundance."

In order to satisfy man with an animal life, the Grand Inquisitor must delude him into a conviction of happiness. To achieve this, he intends to give man a purpose in life by supporting his inherent belief in immortality and

God, and, with promises of heavenly and eternal reward, so lead him to a false sense of bliss. The exclusion of suffering, however, would mean the destruction of humanity, as Ivan himself explains to Alyosha: "One should accept lying and deception and lead man consciously to death and destruction; and yet one should deceive them all the way so that they may not notice where they are being led, that the poor blind creatures may at least, on the way, think themselves happy." Ivan himself, thus, admits that the happiness promised mankind by the Grand Inquisitor is only a deception, and in so doing he, even if involuntarily, sides with Christ. This is plain to Alyosha, who exclaims, "Your poem is to praise Jesus, not to blame Him!"

The Grand Inquisitor, in denying man a link with the spiritual world, is determined to destroy human spirit and thought. Deprived of his divine origin, man will lose—in spite of the spurious notions of happiness provided by the Grand Inquisitor—the idea of God and personal immortality. He will view his life only as "a meaningless flash." There will be no further point to a life now devoid of all meaning; therefore no satisfaction will be left save in self-destruction, as it was with Svidrigaylov and Stavrogin. Dostoevsky explains this condition more fully in *The Diary of a Writer*:

> If man loses his belief in immortality, suicide becomes an absolute and inevitable necessity. . . . But the idea of immortality, promising eternal life, binds man closely to the earth. . . . Man's belief in a personal immortality is the only thing which gives point and reason to his life on earth. Without this belief, his bond with the earth loosens, becomes weak and unstable; the loss of life's higher meaning—even if it is felt only as a most subconscious form of depression and ennui—leads him inevitably to suicide.[5]

As Dostoevsky explicitly states, without a belief in personal immortality,

> People will suddenly realize that there is no more life for them; that there is no freedom of spirit, no will, no per-

sonality; that someone has stolen everything from them; that the human way of life has vanished, to be replaced by the bestial way of life, the way of cattle, with this difference, however, that the cattle do not know that they are cattle, whereas men will discover that they have become cattle. . . . And then, perhaps, others will cry to God, "Thou art right, oh Lord! Man lives not by bread alone!" [6]

The Grand Inquisitor, therefore, who contemplates the elimination of what he believes to be the principle of evil in the structure of the world, admits that he sides with Satan. "Listen," he addresses Christ, "we are not with Thee, but with *him*—that is our secret!" His intention will lead man to absolute evil: to death and destruction. The Grand Inquisitor realizes this, but he believes that his substitution of an acceptable myth for painful conscience will be justified, for he will secure for man the happiness denied him by his inability to accept the idea represented by Christ.

Dostoevsky clearly distinguishes this evil from that manifested in Ivan's hallucination of the devil, who says, "I am the 'X' in an equation with one unknown." It appears from this formulation that evil ending in suffering is an integral part of life just as the "X" is of such an equation. Suffering, for Dostoevsky, is not only inherent in man, but it provides the only spur toward a greater consciousness of reality, which in turn engenders the assertion of man's personality. Complete harmony on earth, therefore, is excluded by the existence of suffering. The world, as it is, must have suffering, and man must have his duality, and yet it is possible to strive for harmony on earth.

A dual force, in Dostoevsky's view, is indispensable for the whole of earthly existence. Life on earth is an incessant striving and must be stimulated by the operation of the two opposite forces of good and evil, which manifest themselves also in man as a part of the universe. As Lebedev in *The Idiot* explains to Evgeny Pavlovich, "The laws of self-preservation and self-destruction are equally powerful in humanity. The devil will maintain his domination over mankind for a period of time which is still unknown to us." The hypothesis that these impulses of self-preservation and self-destruction are a part of the dual and fundamental law of the universe which divert man from his "spiritual world" induces Lebedev to ascribe this law to the realm of the devil. But the impulse of self-preservation must be given its due, since it preserves earthly existence, even though it is one of destruction when considered in relation to the "spiritual world."

According to Dostoevsky, since man's physical nature hinders his independent thoughts and distorts his "spiritual world," there can be no paradise and no harmony so long as man must live under earthly conditions. Kirillov expresses a similar viewpoint in his conversation with Shatov: "There are seconds . . . when you suddenly feel the presence of the eternal harmony perfectly attained. It is something not earthly—I do not mean in the sense that it is heavenly—but in that sense that man cannot endure it in his earthly aspect. He must be physically changed or die." This thought occurs again in the following note: "We do not know which form it [eternal harmony] will take, or where it will take place, . . . in which center, whether in the final center, that is, in the bosom of the universal synthesis—God. . . . It will be in general hardly possible to call men human beings; therefore we have not even an idea what kind of beings we shall be." [7]

With the attainment of man's goal, Dostoevsky further claims, human existence will become static. Thus, it will no longer be necessary for man to develop himself, or to await the coming of future generations to attain his goal. The life hitherto known to man will cease to be a life based on perpetual motion. In the same way, Ivan's devil, who represents the principle of evil in human nature, assures Ivan that he, the devil, "in a simple and straightforward way demands [his] own annihilation," but is commanded to live further. "For there would be nothing without me," he says, "if everything on earth were as it should be, then nothing would happen. There

would be no events without me, but there must be events."
Without the negative, destructive principle of the dual
force, which represents one pole of duality—"the indispensable minus"—there would be no phenomena on
earth. While ultimate harmony would be attained, it
would mean simultaneously the end of earthly life as man
knows it.

The same result would be achieved if man could solve
the mystery of life and find an ultimate answer to the
eternal question "why?" so convincingly presented by
Lebyadkin. The devil, referring to this mystery of life, says
to Ivan, "I know, of course, there is a secret in it, but for
nothing in the world will they tell me this secret; for
then, perhaps, seeing the meaning of it, I might shout
'hosanna!'; the indispensable minus would disappear at
once, and good sense would reign supreme throughout
the world. That, of course, would mean the end of everything."

Thus, while the principle of evil which destroys the
"spiritual world" of man is indispensable for the preservation of earthly existence, the complete transition to absolute evil, quite consciously aimed at by the Grand Inquisitor, would exclude the principle of good, resulting ultimately in death and destruction. Even Ivan Karamazov
himself is convinced that his devil—"the 'X' in an equation with one unknown"—is not the Satan mentioned by
the Grand Inquisitor, but "only a devil." Similarly, Ivan
questions Alyosha in one of the drafts, "In what way is he
Satan? He is a devil, simply a devil. I cannot visualize him
as Satan." [8] In a letter to N. A. Lyubimov, Dostoevsky
reasserts his viewpoint by writing, "Please forgive me
my devil. He is only a devil . . . not Satan with his
'singed' wings." [9] It is strange that this important distinc-
tion escaped the attention of some scholars and critics.
D. H. Lawrence, for example, in his article "Preface to
Dostoevsky's *The Grand Inquisitor*," states forthrightly:
"As always in Dostoevsky, the amazing perspicacity is
mixed with ugly perversity. Nothing is pure. His wild love
for Jesus is mixed with perverse and poisonous hate of

Jesus: his moral hostility to the devil is mixed with secret worship of the devil." [10] It is evident that D. H. Lawrence has overlooked the dichotomy so important for Dostoevsky between Satan and the devil. As has been shown, the Russian novelist equates the devil with "the 'X' in an equation with one unknown," and with "the indispensable minus" in the structure of the world.

The principle of evil is a prerequisite of earthly existence, but Dostoevsky, through Father Zosima, states his view that only the "spiritual world," the "higher part of man's being" can be the goal of human aspiration. The contradictions discussed above, which are characteristic of Dostoevsky's philosophy and are reflected in his fiction, the writer reconciles very forcefully and lucidly.

6 THE SPIRITUAL GOAL

AFTER ANALYZING man's creaturely being as the reflection of metaphysical realities, Dostoevsky, with all the evidence before him, begins to investigate the function of human duality. He comes to the paradoxical conclusion that the metaphysical background of man's continual struggle against his neighbor is a striving for ultimate perfection. This aspiration, Dostoevsky believes, causes nation to fight against nation. As this struggle underlies the history of mankind, Dostoevsky claims that the striving for spiritual perfection is the driving force in the development of mankind and the reason for man's duality. In many of his works, the writer analyzes the following problem: Is man's spiritual and moral perfection an end in itself? This question emerges from Arkady Dolgoruky's meditations on virtue. He is overwhelmed by the thought that, while struggling for his ideal, man is exposed to death, which reduces spiritual perfection to nought, thus making the whole process quite meaningless. There does not seem to be any reason why man should strive for "something completely different," as the Underground Man formulates it if tomorrow life is to be extinguished.

To counterbalance this apparent absurdity, Dostoevsky considers that man must have something absolute, something fundamental to alleviate these doubts concerning the meaning of existence. He must have something to live for, something to serve as a guide for his conduct in life. He needs an assurance of something permanent, for though "man loves chaos and destruction," as the Underground Man maintains, he also longs for a belief in an absolute value, as Ivan Karamazov asserts. This consideration brings Dostoevsky to a hypothesis which he tests and tries to substantiate in many of his writings, and which subsequently becomes his firm conviction. It is his belief that only eternal life can impart meaning and purpose to man's aspiration for spiritual perfection: "Immortality, which promises eternal life, binds man to earth all the more. . . . Only through faith in immortality can man perceive the whole reasonable purpose of life upon earth." [1] Only a lofty idea of immortality, thus, can fill life with content and meaning: "All other sublime ideas of life . . . *are merely derived from this one idea.*" [2] Without this idea, Dostoevsky maintains, man is unable to retain his divine image and consequently cannot live in a way befitting such a noble creature. The novelist writes,

> For me personally, one of the things which fill me with the greatest apprehensions for our future—even our near future—is the fact that, in my view . . . there is spreading with ever-increasing rapidity complete disbelief in the soul and immortality. And not only does this disbelief strengthen itself into a kind of conviction . . . but also into some strange universal indifference that at times even scoffs at this, the loftiest idea of human existence. God knows by virtue of what law it spreads among us. It is indifference not only toward this particular idea, but toward everything else that generates and sustains life, that brings health, that saves us from our own fetid decay. . . . Neither man nor nation can exist without a sublime idea.[3]

To preserve man from the danger of "fetid decay," Dostoevsky searches for a path for man to follow so that he might elude this peril. In this search he arrives at the conclusion that happiness on earth lies in the process of approaching the goal, and not in the goal itself. Should man ever attain it, he would reach something immutable, liable neither to change nor further development: "*Hap-*

piness lies not in happiness itself, but in its pursuit, for with its attainment tedium and anguish ensue; everything has been accomplished—there is nothing more to accomplish; everything is known—there is nothing more to know." [4] Ippolit mentions in his confession that "Columbus was happy, not when he discovered America, but while he was on the way to discovering it." For Dostoevsky, happiness is in striving; living and striving are synonymous.

The dual force of the universe—a force of good and a force of evil—impels man to aspire to a goal, but simultaneously prevents him from attaining it. The Underground Man ponders:

> Man loves to create and to pave the way—of that there can be no question—but why does he also love so passionately to bring about destruction and chaos? . . . Perhaps because he himself is instinctively afraid of attaining his goal, . . . and so bringing to an end his constructive aspirations? . . . Perhaps he loves to see the edifice which he is erecting only from a distance, not from close at hand? . . . And, who knows, perhaps the aim which mankind strives for upon earth is contained solely in this ceaseless continuation of the process of attainment—that is to say, in the living of life rather than in the aim itself, which of course is nothing but the formula that twice two make four. Yes, gentlemen, this formula is not life at all, but the beginning of death.

Man must strive to attain his goal, Dostoevsky contends, for only in this way can he live life to the fullest. He must make his own discoveries in God's creation in order to establish contact with God. "God took seeds from different worlds," Father Zosima teaches, "and sowed them on this earth. Everything which could, came up. His garden grew; but everything which lives and grows does so only through its feeling of contact with other mysterious worlds. If that feeling grows weak or is destroyed in you, the heavenly growth also dies. Then you will be indifferent to life and grow to hate it."

If man, Dostoevsky warns, alienates himself from his

native land, or loses contact with the people to whom he belongs by birth, then this feeling "of contact with other mysterious worlds" grows weak, or is destroyed in him. Thus a curious offshoot of Dostoevsky's dual concept of the world is his Slavophilism, with its underlying "passionate, . . . ecstatic and beautiful love for the Russian soil." [5] He identifies the feeling of nationalism, the passionate love for "Russia, the Mother, the Wife, the Sister," [6] with a positive spiritual quality in a Russian. If he lacks it, he severs himself from his native soil and loses his spirituality. The writer interprets man's estrangement from his country as the last and most decisive stage in the drama of man, and claims that alienation from God would be the logical outcome of such a detachment.

Dostoevsky's nationalism is particularly clear in his concept, itself philosophical, of the Russian soil. To his way of thinking, the soil not only produces the beauty of Russia and the fruits of her labor, but is the one element that ties all Russians together in the sight of God. About himself he says that without the Russian earth his strength and his talent would dry up.[7] People must be bound to their soil, he insists, and in this lies the true foundation of their life. Their native soil, which nurtures them and to which they devote their vital energy, governs their aims upon earth and gives an added meaning to their earthly lives. Man derives from his common heritage a feeling of brotherhood and looks upon his native soil as his mother because it gives him nourishment. "The sense of universal fellowship with all creatures, so characteristic of Dostoevsky's novels," W. Hubben writes, "clearly has its roots in this love for the soil, this precious Russian soil." [8] L. Zander remarks that Dostoevsky's concept of the earth is that it is "the primary reality out of which we are created, by which we live and into which we return. In that sense, the earth is a constituent element of all that lives, the matter out of which it is made." [9] With this same interpretation of the earth in mind, Prince Myshkin says, "He who has no soil of his own also has no God," and Sonya Marmeladov, who has close ties with her soil, advises Raskolnikov to kiss the ground in the hope that he may restore a bond with his native soil and so find his way back to God. Shatov, in an attempt to show Stavrogin that the bond with the earth is indispensable for man's conception of good and evil as well as for his idea of God, counsels him to work as a peasant, because peasants are more closely related to the soil.

This cult of the Russian common people is explicitly expressed in Dostoevsky's journalistic writings: "We must bend down before the Russian common people and expect from them our salvation, our thought and action. We must bow down before their truth and accept it as our own." [10] He constantly appeals to the Russian intelligentsia to stop looking down upon the common people as mentally underdeveloped. Much can be learned from them, the novelist insists, because they know good from evil and have a clear idea of what Christ means to the individual and to mankind. "Revive and strengthen the root of the spirit of the Russian common people," Dostoevsky writes, "this root is great in its spiritual significance. This root is the beginning of everything." [11]

The work in which Dostoevsky develops these ideas is *The Possessed*. The central character, Nikolay Stavrogin, who provides the initial impetus for all events in the novel, is a man who has been torn from his native soil and thus deprived of the feeling of unity with his fellow men. For Stavrogin, religion and the consciousness of belonging to a nation go together, as can be seen from his own words: "An atheist at once ceases to be a Russian." Shortly before his suicide, he professes in a letter to Dasha to take heed of her brother's words: "The man who loses connection with his soil, loses his gods: that is, he loses his aims." A stranger in his own country, Stavrogin admits in this farewell letter, "I have no ties in Russia —everything there is just as alien to me as it is elsewhere."

Stavrogin has just as strong a will to live as other men, but, Dostoevsky implies, it is rendered impotent by his disbelief in immortality. This impotence is a natural outcome of his alienation from his fellow countrymen. Devoid of a bond with the Russian soil and the Russian people, he cannot find the way back to them because he cannot distinguish good from evil in his emotional life, a differentiation which is ultimately linked to man's belief in immortality. A failure to develop such a belief deprives him of a purpose in life, and thus his will to live grows weaker. There is no organic unity in him as a "mixture of the heavenly and earthly," and his spiritual nature remains sterile. Unable to utilize the power of his spirit anywhere, he aimlessly seeks an outlet which will bring him contentment, but he is doomed to continual failure: "I have tried my power everywhere," he writes Dasha, "you advised me to do this 'that I might learn to know myself.' . . . This power appears infinite . . . but to what to apply my power, that is what I have never seen." Shatov directs him to kiss the ground and to water it with tears. "Get to know God by work . . . by work on the land," he counsels him, but Stavrogin fears that the unguided use of his power in such labors would not of itself be sufficient to bring him to a knowledge of God any more than it would suffice to conquer his egocentricity and feeling of shame. He is not strong enough to give up the gratification of his creaturely being; nor can he restore the bond with his native soil and with the Russians, a bond which might have compelled him to abandon his easy life as the idle son of a squire, with all its worldly pleasures. His life becomes gradually more and more void of meaning until finally he finds himself in a blind alley.

Divorce from the people, idleness and boredom, the confusion of moral criteria, a cold and rational intellect, disbelief in immortality, subservience to his creaturely being, and indulgence in sensual experiences as an attempt to find a "way out," reduce Stavrogin's will to live to nought and result in his ultimate spiritual disintegration. His very strength is atrophied by his inability to redeem sin through suffering and thereby to know God and to believe in immortality.

To avoid spiritual disintegration by becoming a prey to his baser impulses and to keep in sight his spiritual goal, man must, Dostoevsky claims, beside retaining close connection with his native soil, strive together with his fellow men for moral self-betterment. In Dostoevsky's opinion, man, regardless of his individual attitude toward life, strives subconsciously for spiritual self-perfection, which is the loftiest ideal and the highest goal of humanity. His innate desire for harmony compels him to seek it. "Individual self-perfection is not only '*the beginning* of everything,' but also its continuation and end. It—and it alone —embraces, creates and preserves the national organism." [12] As man's individual bliss is dependent upon national unity and united effort, he needs the companionship of others in order to aspire to spiritual perfection. "It is for the sake of individual self-perfection that the social structure of a nation exists, since it came into being only for the preservation of an initially acquired treasure." [13] Man seeks to find in this communion with his fellow men a support and protection for his own striving. "Personal immortality and God are one and the same, an identical idea," [14] writes Dostoevsky to one of his friends. From this conviction grows the idea that striving for God and immortality is the primary cause of the genesis of nations: "The object of every national movement, in every people and at every period of its existence, is only seeking for a god who must be its own god, and the faith in him as the only true god. God is the synthetic personality of the whole people, taken from its beginning to its end," Shatov points out to Stavrogin.

For Dostoevsky, then, religion is also closely related to the problem of duality insofar as it is the product of man's spiritual being. Emerging from the idea of spiritual self-perfection, religion imparts meaning to human life and leads man to his ideal. On the other hand, as the Grand Inquisitor explains to Christ, religion is the cause of strife among nations, a strife which impedes the progress of humanity to universal brotherhood. As a stimulus to man's triumphant progress toward his ultimate goal, religion has for Dostoevsky great metaphysical significance. It has the power to foster man's aspiration for spiritual self-betterment, but only when his moral ideal is founded on the original notion of good and evil held by a particular people. "Every nation has its own conception of good and evil as well as its own good and evil," Shatov observes.

The duality of religion thus engenders another dual phenomenon—nations' striving for universal harmony and simultaneously struggling with one another. This struggle prevents them from attaining their goal. Developing the view that the concept of good and evil held by a group of people is the actual origin of a nation, Dostoevsky makes the following statement:

> Invariably and everywhere these beliefs assumed the form of religion, the form of a confession of the new idea. Just as soon as a new religion came into being, a new civic nationality came into existence. Look at the Hebrews and Mohammedans: Jewish nationality came into being after the Mosaic law, but its beginning can be traced to the law of Abraham, while the Mohammedan nationalities arose only after the Koran was written. In order to preserve the acquired spiritual heritage, men are forthwith attracted to each other, and only then do they zealously and anxiously, 'working *beside each other, one for another, and with the other*' . . . begin to investigate how they should organize themselves so as to preserve the heritage without losing any part of it, and how they might find a *civic* formula of common existence to help them to promote the acquired moral treasure in its full glory throughout the world.[15]

The civic formula of life, Dostoevsky believes, is the fundamental structure of a community, its basis and social order. It is formed according to national ideals and corresponds only to one particular nation. An alien social order or form of civilization cannot harmonize with the national aspirations of another country, with its concept of good and evil, its moral ideals, or the community structure through which the people strive to express their ideal. The mere adoption of an alien moral code will arouse no response in the "spiritual world" of another nation because of the difference in their moral ideals. A nation which accepts the ready-made ideals of another nation without having passed through all the phases necessary to acquire these ideals naturally may even become distorted and warped in its nature. This, Dostoevsky fears, may be the future of his own country, burdened with the notions and doctrines of the West which are so extraneous to the natural characteristics of the Russian. Notions of honor and duty, springing from the structure of a nation, can even be good or evil in themselves, but "this is only a secondary question," Arkady Dolgoruky's former tutor writes; "what is of most consequence is the finality and completeness of the forms, and with this the existence of at least some sort of order, not prescribed from above, but developed from within. Good heavens, what matters most of all for us is to have at least some sort of order of our own!"

The acceptance of suffering, another cardinal point in Dostoevsky's philosophy, is intimately connected with the problem of duality. In his search for a righteous life, man must be blessed with meekness and humility. In accepting suffering, he develops positive traits of his character and gradually frees himself of the uncertain and tormenting delusions of earthly life. Dostoevsky clearly distinguishes physical from spiritual suffering: Father Zosima writes in his exhortations, "They talk of hell fire in the material sense. . . . I think if there were fire in the material sense they would be glad of it, for I imagine that in material agony, even if only for a moment, their still greater spiritual agony would be forgotten; but spiritual agony cannot be taken from them, for that is not external: it is within them." Dostoevsky is mainly interested in spiritual suffering, for he is more concerned with man's soul than with his physical life.

The metaphysical significance which Dostoevsky attaches to suffering is revealed in "The Legend of the Grand Inquisitor." The Grand Inquisitor's Christ has chosen for man "all that is exceptional, vague, and enigmatic" and "burdened him with suffering forever" not because of His lack of love for man, but because, in the

Underground Man's expression, suffering is not only inherent in man but "is the sole cause of the awakening of consciousness." Christ does not propose to spare people anything. He leaves them to bear all the pain of human existence. He wants them to decide for themselves the direction of their development: whether to strive for spiritual self-perfection, or to gratify the desires and passions of their natural being. For this purpose man has been endowed with spiritual capacities: "All has been vouchsafed to man by God's will," Makar Dolgoruky says to Arkady. "Not for nothing did the Lord breathe into him the breath of life; and not for nothing did He give him the commandment 'live and learn!' " Man must surrender to "all that is exceptional, vague, and enigmatic," he must suffer, for only with suffering comes the realization that he is a being created in God's image. Toward this point, the highest peak of consciousness, man's striving is directed. "What is life?" Dostoevsky asks in a draft of *The Brothers Karamazov:* "The most pertinent definition of 'Self' is, I am, I exist in order to be like the Sovereign Who says, 'I am He Who is, and I exist in the whole universe in its completion and entirety.' Then to give up everything . . . as God freely gives up everything and then to return to Him (the Logos), and to find Him again: this is life." [16]

Dostoevsky's conviction that, in order to attain full consciousness of reality at its highest level, man must accept the suffering that results from his dual nature is expressed in many of his novels. Dmitry Karamazov experiences real existence when he is on the point of accepting wholeheartedly the tribulations imposed upon him by his confession of his father's murder, of which he is not guilty. He longs to suffer since this will enable him to repeat to himself every moment, "I exist! In thousands of agonies—I exist! I am tormented on the rack—but I exist!" The whole character of his dual being, with all the Karamazov passions, lust and sensuality on the one hand, and on the other with a spirit striving for perfection, is revealed to him only when he comprehends the meaning of suffering and consequently knows it to be justified. He realizes that only through his own suffering can he plumb the reality of his own being, for suffering brings about the co-ordination of his "spiritual world" and his natural being. He can synthesize these two realities only through mental agony. In his belief that he is ready to accept suffering, Dmitry feels happy, and faces for the first time the reality of his existence, which was previously hidden from him. "During these last two months I have found in myself a new man. A new man has risen up within me! He was hidden from me, he would never have come to the surface, if it had not been for this blow from Heaven!" Through his trials, Dmitry experiences the reality of God and at the same time the reality of his own being. In a similar way, Sonya Marmeladov's suffering proves to her that she cannot exist without God.

The greatness of suffering, in Father Zosima's opinion, "lies in the fact that it is a mystery, that in it the passing earthly show and the eternal truth are brought together." Therefore, a world created by God without suffering would have been a useless and ineffectual vacuum. Happiness without sorrow, the end to which the Grand Inquisitor intends to lead man, is an illusion. Real happiness upon earth, for Dostoevsky, is the consciousness of existence which man can attain only through suffering. In a draft of *Crime and Punishment* Dostoevsky writes,

> Man is not born for happiness. He earns his happiness only through suffering. There is no injustice in this, as living knowledge and consciousness, experienced directly through man's body and soul and through the whole process of living, can be acquired only by a frank examination of the foundations of his beliefs. He will acquire his contentment only by spiritual anguish, for the law of our planet will have it this way. This direct consciousness which is experienced through the process of living is a great joy for which one must pay with years of misery, without regret.[17]

"There is no happiness in well-being. Happiness is gained only through suffering."[18] This is reiterated by Dostoevsky in a letter to S. A. Ivanova, in which he says,

"Man, without suffering, cannot even understand happiness, for one's ideal passes through suffering like gold passes through fire. The Kingdom of Heaven can be attained only through and with an effort." [19]

Ivan's double, his devil, also maintains that "suffering is life." Paradoxically enough, the appearance of the devil signifies Ivan's search for truth through "spiritual agony." In the name of humanity, Ivan refuses to accept God's creation with its pain, injustice and evil. As his rebellion against God is based on a desire for some justification of the senseless misery of human existence, denial of God should have been for him the logical result of this attitude. He should have denied God as does the Grand Inquisitor. However, it is not God Whom Ivan denies; it is God's creation which he cannot accept, and it is in consequence of this denial that Ivan's devil appears before him, manifesting Ivan's acceptance of spiritual torment. Although with his reason Ivan may protest against human misery in general, subconsciously he is seeking it in the same way as Stavrogin. Alyosha, aware of this, says to Rakitin, "It is not money, it is not comfort Ivan is seeking. Perhaps it is suffering he is seeking." Ivan seeks suffering in order to acquire knowledge and understanding of God and His creation. He envies Dmitry's willingness to sing hymns to God, this being the expression of Dmitry's consciousness of reality. Filled with the desire to experience his older brother's delight, Ivan is prepared "to give a quadrillion quadrillions for two seconds of joy."

The tragic figure of the Grand Inquisitor, whose actions are motivated by love for his "feeble neighbor," shows the extent of Ivan's agony. The latter meditates on the problems put forward in "The Legend" and struggles toward the acceptance of divine justice. When the Grand Inquisitor presents the case for the denial of God, in which he disavows Christ's teaching because of the existence of suffering, Christ remains silent. This silence indicates His inability to refute the Grand Inquisitor's charges. On the other hand, the Grand Inquisitor himself knows that in advocating the elimination of suffering, he is siding with Satan, by whom come death and destruction. Thus the Grand Inquisitor denies man every hope of experiencing those joys for which Ivan would give "a quadrillion quadrillions." This hope for joy, and for escape from the death and destruction which Satan brings, speaks then in favor of human sorrow, while the profound feeling of pity and compassion for man speak against it. When Ivan examines the pros and cons of suffering, he constantly vacillates between belief and disbelief. On this hinges all his tragic agony, for as Father Zosima explains to him, "In you this problem has not been solved, and this is your great grief, for it clamors for an answer."

Stavrogin also would have escaped the void "beyond good and evil," and the aimlessness of life, if he could have accepted suffering, as Tikhon advises. He confesses that "he looks for infinite pain"; he even asks Tikhon not to dissuade him from this search, because otherwise he will "sink into committing atrocities." Yet Tikhon's advice to live for five or seven years as a hermit in order to repent his sin and to suffer, is not even given consideration. Thus, when Stavrogin has a chance to endure mental tribulations, he refuses, too weak to sacrifice his voluntary self-deceptions for the sake of truth, or to accept the suffering which his conscience compels him to seek.

In view of the importance of suffering in human life, Dostoevsky, searching for its fullest meaning, endeavors to penetrate and fathom its depth in Christ, the greatest being who ever lived upon the earth—He Who suffered most, and for all. Christ accepted His torments without resistance and without a feeling of anger toward His torturers. In the hour of crucifixion, He cried to God, "Father, forgive them; for they know not what they do!" He had come to deliver the world by His suffering, to redeem men from their sins, and to atone for the agony and tears of the innocent. While on earth, He called upon man to take up his cross for the love of his fellows, and to follow Him. He took it upon Himself to show mankind the path of unlimited suffering for the love of humanity,

of the earth, and of life—love which ultimately prevented Him from descending from the cross. It was this
love which made Him accept His final agony and reveal
to man the essence of life. Christ could suffer because He
"was made flesh." Although He, "the only begotten of
the Holy Spirit," was connected with the spiritual
world as no human being before Him or after, He had at
the same time bodily form. The suffering which brings
together "the passing earthly show and the eternal truth,"
thus makes Christ the noblest and loftiest being ever to
live upon earth.

In life, Dostoevsky emphasizes, man must endeavor
to follow the example of Christ, His meekness, love, and
obedience unto death. Besides retaining spiritual connection with his native land and his fellows, man must then,
in his striving for moral perfection, accept "spiritual
agony" in the Christ-like way, for only thus can he
acquire humility and tolerance. Therefore, Dostoevsky's
appeal, "Believe in the spirit of the people; from it alone
expect your salvation, and you will be saved," [20] points the
way to the deliverance of mankind from evil. Adherence
to the moral ideas of one's native land leads to moral
self-betterment, preserves the "acquired treasure" and
gives, at the same time, through the common bond of
the native soil, the possibility of accepting suffering.

The characters in Dostoevsky who accept spiritual
pain ignore completely their own selfish desires and, in
so doing, experience life in all its fullness, and come to
spiritual perfection. They are willing to bear their burden
and accept their destiny unresistingly. In their lives they
are moved not by intellectual reasoning but by feeling,
as Christ was when He died for men on the cross. "Everyone in the world understands, or at least can understand,
that one *should love one's neighbor as oneself*. As a matter
of fact, the whole meaning of human life is contained in
this knowledge, as Christ told us. This knowledge is inherent in man, bestowed upon him gratuitously, for our
intellect can by no means give us such comprehension.
And why not? It is simply because it is unreasonable 'to

love one's neighbor' if one is to judge by reason," [21] writes Dostoevsky. The logic of reason can never do complete justice to the living of life, or as Razumikhin in *Crime and Punishment* says, "You cannot jump over human nature by logic alone! Logic can only foresee three possibilities, but there are a whole million of them!" Reason, science, empirical thought cannot penetrate to the core of life, but intuition can, for it is rooted in the universe: "Man on earth is hidden from us," Father Zosima claims, "but to make up for that, we have been endowed with a mystic and inborn sense of our living bond with the other world, with the higher heavenly world; and the roots of our thoughts and feelings are not here, but in other worlds. That is why the philosophers say that we cannot comprehend the reality of things on earth."

Inspired by the desire for service and for self-sacrifice, and by giving himself up for others, man gains the greatest freedom—that of personal will. In *Winter Notes on Summer Impressions* Dostoevsky writes, "A voluntary, completely conscious sacrifice for the benefit of all others is, in my opinion, the sign of the highest development of the human personality, its greatest source of power and its greatest self-control: it is the sign of the greatest freedom of the individual will. To lay down one's life for one's fellow men, to die for them on the cross, or to ascend the funeral pyre, can be achieved only by one with the highest development of personality." Dostoevsky considers this development the goal of man's striving, and believes that earthly life exists only for the purpose of man's development toward perfection. Therefore Christ, Who reveals the possibility of this perfection, is for Dostoevsky the manifestation of man's highest development. In Dostoevsky's writings, there is a significant passage which throws more light on his thoughts on Christ:

> After Christ's appearance *as the ideal of mankind in the flesh*, it becomes as clear as daylight that the highest and most final development of the personality . . . will be reached when man consciously attains his goal, and is convinced with the whole vitality of his nature that the highest

use he can make of his personality—his fully developed ego—is to find a way to destroy that ego and to sacrifice it completely for the benefit of all. This is the greatest happiness. In this way the law of the individual ego flows together with the law of humanity. In the confluence, both of them, the individual ego as well as the whole of humanity—seemingly two extreme antitheses—while destroying each other, attain simultaneously and separately the highest goal of their individual development.[22]

This brings the argument back to Shatov's assertion concerning duality—that mankind is moved by "the force of an insatiable desire to go on to the end, though at the same time it denies that end. It is the force of the persistent assertion of one's own existence, and a denial of death." Dostoevsky, who attributes great import to the force which prevents man from attaining his highest development, seems at the same time to be convinced that man will ultimately succeed. The importance of this force which prevents man from ever attaining his goal is the fact that its absence—like the absence of "the 'X' in the equation with one unknown"—would mean the end of earthly life, as Ivan's devil has so clearly stated. For Dostoevsky, earthly life represents the transitory state in which man resists going to the end so long as he is not sufficiently mature for "the final stage of his development."

Ivan is overwhelmed by this contradiction in human nature, and through his Grand Inquisitor poses a question: Why is man created in such a way that he will seek the gratification of his "flesh and lust," when he is able to find real happiness only in self-abnegation? The answer is to be found in Dostoevsky's assertion: "Upon earth man strives for an ideal which contradicts his very nature. If he does not obey the law prompting him to strive for his ideal, does not sacrifice his ego for love of his fellow human beings, he suffers and calls this condition 'sin.' Man must suffer continually but this will be recompensed by the joys of paradise brought about by the fulfillment of the law. In this lies the earthly equilibrium. Otherwise life upon earth would be meaningless." [23] Man would have little possibility of spiritual suffering if he were not, simultaneously with his moral striving, drawn away from his goal by his search for comfort and physical well-being. Without his struggling, he would be deprived of the chance to strive for the highest perfection of his personality: there would be no need for further suffering or striving, and he would have lapsed into a state of apathy. However, God considered man worthy of pursuing a high goal, as a being created in the divine image, who seeks to achieve consciousness at its highest level and to be like his God, Who says, "I am He Who is." This goal attained, all the contradictions would automatically melt away. A paradise on earth would be established.

The question of the Kingdom of Heaven on earth in Dostoevsky's work is closely related to the problem of universal duality. He admits that he has no definite ideas of what form the future paradise on earth will take, but he feels that one of its main characteristics will be the disappearance of man's duality. The complexity of Dostoevsky's thought concerning a paradise on earth can be summed up in the following argument: when man attains the ideal state, his impulse for self-preservation will naturally vanish, and the result will be the disappearance of the human reproductive instinct, bringing mankind's ultimate extinction. But the phenomenon of duality is an indispensable prerequisite for man's achievement of his own individual spiritual perfection. He can arrive at this goal only through the full development of his personality, that is, by experiencing, however painfully, the situations arising from his dual nature. In this striving, he is condemned to suffer because, in the face of his duality, his efforts appear to be futile. He is afraid, as the young Zosima says to his mysterious visitor, that his ideal existence on earth can never be anything but a dream so long as man is isolated from man by selfish human greed. This realization, however, does not contradict Dostoevsky's firm belief that universal brotherhood is the goal of humanity, and that man, despite his ordeals, must strive toward this goal.

In "The Dream of a Ridiculous Man," Dostoevsky states that if man abandoned the egocentricity which forces him to cling to his creaturely being, he could immediately transform the earth into a paradise. The Ridiculous Man insists that "in one day, *in one hour*, everything would be arranged! It is important to love others as yourself. That is of major importance; it is everything, nothing else is wanted: you will find out immediately how to arrange it all. . . . If only everyone wants it, it can all be arranged right away." On the other hand, however, this paradise is not possible because of the existence of evil, "the 'X' in the equation with one unknown"; yet the Ridiculous Man is resolved to preach paradise on earth. "Even supposing this paradise never comes to pass (and I do understand that this cannot be otherwise!)," he says, "yet I shall go on preaching it."

In this statement is the key to Dostoevsky's philosophy: though paradise on earth is unattainable so long as man is burdened by his dual nature, the aspiration for it is quite possible and highly desirable because it imparts to man the power to develop "the higher, spiritual world" of his personality, and gives a purpose to his life. As the principle of evil is indispensable to the preservation of earthly existence, Dostoevsky does not challenge man to ignore it wholly in the pursuit of his goal, but rather to modify its influence by the greater development of his spiritual life. The Christ of the Grand Inquisitor does not relieve man of his dual nature, of the worry associated with his daily bread, or of the pain of his stricken conscience: all this is necessary for man to attain paradise in the world to come. The exercise of man's freedom of conscience implies suffering and struggling, but in this striving for the spiritual goal Dostoevsky sees the meaning of human life and of man's victory over his creaturely nature. In order to do justice to the "spiritual world," man must not be content to subject himself to the control of a dictatorial authority, nor must he seek satisfaction only in the earthly aspects of life. Although unable to free himself entirely from his selfish instincts, he must never abandon his striving for freedom from them.

To Dostoevsky, faith in God and immortality are synonymous with a meaning in life and man's striving for an ultimate goal. "How is man going to be virtuous without God?" Dmitry asks Alyosha. "How is he to know, without God, what is virtue, and what is not? After all, what is virtue? . . . Virtue is one thing for me, another for a Chinese; consequently it is a relative thing." Without God, man can have only conventional virtues, and no absolute ones. Without God, Dmitry feels he cannot endure. "One cannot exist in prison without God," he claims, "it is even more impossible than out of prison." He fears that "the new man" within him and his will to suffer may leave him again if he has no faith in God.

The problems of faith and disbelief constitutes another aspect of Dostoevsky's emphasis on duality: if faith in God and in immortality is so indispensable to human existence, why is man given the possibility of questioning them? Dostoevsky's answer is that an automatic, innate faith in God, excluding doubt, would bar man from attaining the consciousness of himself as a being made in the divine image. If faith in God were not subject to doubt, man would be deprived of spiritual torment and this would result in an inability ever to attain full consciousness; he would become simply another form of matter, unaware of its existence. In this concept is contained the significance of Christ's martyrdom: He refused to descend from the cross, for "He did not want to convert people *forcibly* through an external miracle, but desired *freedom of spirit*." [24] The only people who do not question the justice of God in Dostoevsky's works are those who, by their very temperament, accept suffering without resistance and, like Job, are ready to take up their predestined cross. For their belief in God, they have paid in the coin of the misery which they joyfully endure. Praising His righteousness, they suffer without question, whereas other people, the ones reluctant to bear their burden, or those not destined to suffer much, must doubt

God and His justice. For these, however, there is divine compensation, for the grace of God is contained in these agonizing doubts.

In Ivan Karamazov, who may serve as an example of the latter, the close relationship between his denial and his simultaneous affirmation of God and His creation is shown in masterly fashion. When Ivan wonders if his unbearable doubt will ever disappear, Father Zosima retorts, "You should thank the Creator Who has given you a lofty heart capable of such suffering, of thinking, and of seeking higher truths, for our dwelling is in the Heavens." "A convinced atheist stands one step beneath the perfect faith—even if he never attains it—whereas an indifferent man has no faith whatever," says Tikhon to Stavrogin. Dostoevsky's atheist is a martyr who torments himself with his continual doubt of God. In this way, he accepts suffering and stands close to the great joy of perfect faith. As he is a man who has the will to suffer, he is on the way to the goal of humanity, spiritual self-perfection.

Accepting suffering, as Christ did, means a complete renunciation of human selfishness. Even for Him it cost much, since He too "was made flesh." Even He tried to evade His great suffering when He entreated God, "O my Father, if it is possible, let this cup pass from me." Man, much weaker than Christ, is capable of bearing the burden only in proportion to his degree of spiritual development. "Heavy burdens are not for all men—for some they are impossible," Alyosha consoles Dmitry, when the latter fails to bear his burden with composure, but Dostoevsky himself insists that every man is capable of accepting suffering, if not in its fullness then at least to a degree which makes him honest with himself and aware of his own sins and shortcomings. The writer claims that the way to man's spiritual self-perfection begins with the acceptance of the truth for which the Grand Inquisitor considers man to be too weak, and with the avowal of man's real nature. In this way man can regain his lost faith in God.

"How can one get back to one's faith?" Liza Kokhlakov's mother asks Father Zosima, who replies, "Above all, avoid falsehood, every kind of falsehood, especially falsehood to yourself. Be on guard against your own falsehood and look into it every hour, every minute." Like Tolstoy, Dostoevsky is of the opinion that human falsehood is at the root of man's distorted and twisted nature. In Tolstoy's "The Death of Ivan Ilyich," the hero realizes on his deathbed the falsity of the life he has lived, and that that falsity has been his master. In a similar way, Dostoevsky's Ridiculous Man recognizes the falsity of human life in his dream: "People learnt to lie, grew fond of lying, and discovered the charm of falsehood. . . . That germ of falsity made its way into their hearts and pleased them. Then sensuality was soon begotten, sensuality begot jealousy, jealousy cruelty. . . . Very soon the first blood was shed. . . . They become so jealous of their own rights that they did their very utmost to curtail and destroy those of others, and made that the chief thing in their lives." [25]

Man should not live by self-deception; he should be constantly aware of his true nature. Father Zosima insists that man must learn to discern his own longing to gratify vanity. He appeals to man not to seek to justify his selfish actions by attributing some elevated purpose to them. As The Ridiculous Man maintains, human selfishness can deceive man about the real motives of his actions to such an extent that he will live in falsehood. Endowing himself with imaginary virtues, he will believe that the deeds performed to gratify his selfish inclinations and feed his vanity spring from highly idealistic intentions. Dostoevsky's first prerequisite for spiritual perfection is that man must know himself, which he cannot do until he stops lying to himself and others. To become the master of his own egocentricity, man must accept the truth about himself.

If man is to know what is right and what is wrong, he should not allow logic to dominate feeling and intuition, nor should he base his judgments entirely on opinions which he has adopted from others. Convictions which are the result of man's logical thinking alone cannot lead to self-knowledge, because they are devoid of the moral foundation which comes from feeling. Convinced that he is an unselfish "friend of humanity," ready to sacrifice himself for the sake of others and quite disinterested in profit, he could, in certain circumstances, become a criminal. "Love of humanity" of the Malthusian type is the result of rational reasoning:

> A man's conduct may be honest, but his actions nevertheless may be immoral. If they conform only to his convictions, they need not be moral. Sometimes it is even more moral not to act in accordance with one's own belief, as some people have shown. Although remaining absolutely loyal to their persuasions, they often do not carry out their intentions because of their feeling. Man reproaches and despises himself for this failure, but his feeling, that is, his conscience, does not allow him to carry out his actions. . . . He abandons his adherence to his convictions only because he considers it more moral than following the voice of reason.[26]

If man relies on his intuition, he is able to see the real motive for his action, and is consequently not easily tempted into self-deception. If feeling dominates reason, his actions are infallible.

The way to self-knowledge involves much suffering, for in order to conquer one's shortcomings—such as a propensity to falsehood, cowardice, vanity, and a desire to prevail over others—one must acknowledge them openly. Dostoevsky maintains that there is no greater difficulty for man than to be honest with himself. "The hardest thing in life," maintains Stepan Trofimovich Verkhovensky in *The Possessed*, "is to live without telling lies . . . and without believing in one's own lies."

There are characters in Dostoevsky's work who, by following a hard path, attain truth. They grasp the meaning of suffering and find bliss and happiness in their almost insufferable pain. Other characters, who have no courage to face the truth and to suffer for its sake, lapse into a spiritually comatose state, unhappy and in isolation from others. Dostoevsky portrays this condition in Golyadkin, who, too fearful to attain truth by accepting suffering, loses his significance as a human being and exists only in a creaturely state. Therefore, the two realities, the "earthly show" and the "eternal truth," which, as Father Zosima insists, should be brought together in suffering, do not acquire any meaning for Golyadkin. The result is his alienation from reality and consequently from the object of human life.

Like Golyadkin, Polzunkov, the hero of Dostoevsky's short story of the same name, feels that he is more insignificant than his fellow men. The narrator of the story sees him relating one of his experiences to an audience. Polzunkov appears in it in a ridiculous light, as spiritually empty, the victim of a cold-blooded egotist. None of the people to whom he tells his story realize that there is courage and a certain heroism in the way he makes himself a target for their disdain and mockery, but Polzunkov himself is suddenly struck by the thought that "he is perhaps more honest than many of these respected people." He is both amazed and amused as he thinks that they, too, probably have similar recollections of appearing ridiculous, but they are not prepared to admit their disgrace, and prefer to laugh at him. This realization brings to Polzunkov a feeling of superiority over his audience, for he does not conceal his vanity, but overcomes shame and admits his weaknesses, and in this way he abandons egoism and becomes "a person with a good heart." He suffers because of their mockery, but this suffering is not useless, as it appears on the surface, for it is only a tiny part of man's great struggle against his egocentricity.

In *Notes from the Underground*, Dostoevsky returns to the theme of martyrdom for truth and the acceptance of suffering. The Underground Man is vain, wicked, cruel, cowardly, and apparently devoid of all positive qualities. In reality, his moral degradation is a stepping-stone to "something quite different," his spiritual self-betterment. There are many people morally depraved, with vanity wounded, Dostoevsky argues, who have no courage to admit their faults even to themselves. They pretend, like Golyadkin, not to be aware of the low state of their morals; and so long as they go on deceiving themselves in this manner, "the spiritual world, the higher part of man's being," is remote and unattainable for them. The Underground Man, however, is brave enough to avow his selfishness and vanity, because he wants to strive for "something quite different." He is not afraid of self-knowledge. "In me," he admits, "fate seems to have combined only the materials for a nonentity." He realizes that all the people around him are base, too, but he feels troubled rather than relieved by his discovery. The tragedy which he shares with his fellow men binds him to them. His mourning for his life is the mourning for their lives; for so long as men support falsehood and self-deception, they remain divorced from reality. "All of us stand divorced from life; all of us halt in a greater or lesser degree. So unfamiliar with reality have we become, that at times we feel a positive loathing for 'real life' and so cannot bear to be reminded of it." The Underground Man is bold enough to admit the truth about himself, and in so doing stands nearer "real life" than the others. With this understanding, he says to the reader, "As for what concerns me in particular, I have in my life only carried to an extreme what you have not dared to carry half-way, and, what is more, you have taken your cowardice for good sense, and have found comfort in deceiving yourself."

An avowal of baseness, such as the Underground Man's, brings man suffering, but this triumph of his "spiritual world" is the bridge which leads him over his "flesh and lust" to truth and reality. Though he hides in his underground like a mouse in its hole, far from reality and from "real life," he is more alive than the people around him. This contradiction is only a seeming one, though. However wicked and selfish the Underground Man may be, he cannot be identified with evil, because he has the courage to bear the burden of conscience. He does not seek to place the responsibility for his actions on someone else;

nor does he endeavor to justify his life by an appeal to some irreproachable authority, such as the Grand Inquisitor suggests. "Come," the Underground Man says mockingly to the reader, "try to give us a little more independence, untie our hands, and we—yes, I assure you that we should start begging to be under control again at once." Man, longing for the Grand Inquisitor's authority, does not want to be made responsible for himself; he is loath to take up the burden of his sin. Therefore, renouncing his spiritual life, he lives for Satan, who brings "death and self-destruction." The Underground Man, who understands human nature all too deeply, admits that he himself lives in the spirit of Satan. But listening to the voice of conscience, he knows his attitude toward life to be evil. Through this avowal, he becomes enlightened and takes the first step toward his spiritual self-perfection, toward "something quite different."

The pawnbroker in "The Gentle Maiden" also has enough courage to own to himself his inherent pride, vanity, and selfishness. Emboldened by this honesty, he now believes himself to be capable of mastering his weaknesses. He is convinced that he is now free from the afflictions weighing heavily upon man, his egocentricity and isolation. These faults have suddenly left him. "The scales have fallen from my eyes," he thinks, and feels that he is about to be freed from his former selfishness. His emancipation from egocentricity takes place at the moment he becomes aware that he no longer means anything to his wife. At this crucial moment he feels a strong desire to discard his egoism and transform his love for himself into love for his wife. Prevented previously by his egocentricity from giving her love, throughout the winter he expected her to come forward offering her love for him, whereupon he would make his response. Now he realizes that one who wishes to give and not take must confer happiness upon others freely, without condition or compulsion. He himself characterizes his former state in the following way: "Before me there hung the scales which blinded my perception. The fateful, disastrous scales!"

Once he realizes that she no longer loves him, he cannot resist a desire to relinquish egoism and give her his love freely. This love, which his pride has so long suppressed, overflows, and he is able to cast off all haughtiness. Ready to forsake self-centeredness entirely, he is filled with an intoxicating feeling of happiness. It seems to him that only at this instant does he begin "to live a real life," to be conscious of himself as a human being. "Rapture was bubbling so in my heart that I thought every moment would be my last . . . although it was coupled with a total understanding of my hopeless despair." This rapture is not even impaired by his clear recognition of her inability to love him further. He reveals everything to her —his egoism, cowardice, vanity, and all the other things which he has been concealing even from himself during his life—and his original plan to conquer his wife, in order to flatter his own vanity, is driven from his mind.

His victory is a great one—a victory over himself—but even this triumph is not complete, as his selfishness does not leave him entirely. He forces upon his wife a confession which she does not wish to hear; his pity and compassion for himself, his rapture and ecstasy of happiness, are his main concern. To have regarded her prayers "to say no more about it and to recall no more memories," he would have been forced to stem the outburst of his feeling, but his transport of delight is too overwhelming to enable him to think about his wife's uneasiness and fear. "I could see that I was wearying her. Do not think me so stupid and egotistical as not to have seen it. I saw everything down to the minutest detail. I saw and was conscious of everything better than anyone else could be," he confessed to himself after her suicide. Though the pawnbroker could perceive his wife's ever-mounting panic, he still continued his outburst thinking only of himself and of his own happiness. Expecting a complete and immediate understanding from his wife, he again thought only of himself. In spite of earnest attempts at self-abnegation, he was unable to accept suffering in full measure, but for a short while he experienced the happiness of one who renounces his own self for the sake of truth.

The Ridiculous Man is permitted to attain this happiness in its fullness. Ashamed of appearing ridiculous, like the pawnbroker in "The Gentle Maiden," he suffers because of egocentricity. But whereas the pawnbroker expects a reward for his self-abnegation, the Ridiculous Man does not even think of such considerations; he just longs to be rid of self for the sake of humanity. Yearning for suffering, he is determined to have his "blood drained to the last drop in these agonies." The refusal of the people in his dream to crucify him, because they do not see his guilty part in their corruption, fills him with pain and sorrow, as he sincerely seeks suffering. He falls asleep with a determination to destroy himself, and awakes with a immeasurable ecstasy in his heart, and an eagerness to live and preach the truth for the rest of his life. Now he neither ponders over his ridiculous appearance, nor does he, like the pawnbroker, complain of the absurdity of life.

"The Dream of a Ridiculous Man" is symbolic of man's renunciation of his selfishness, of the happiness which comes when he is resolved to dedicate his life to others. The actual possibility of this sacrifice, which imparts meaning to man's painful duality, is represented by another group of Dostoevsky's characters, who resemble Christ in their capacity to sacrifice themselves for others.

CRITICS have often designated as the "meek" type the group of characters who show man the way to spiritual perfection in Dostoevsky's fiction. The "meek" man, although he may experience the endless struggle between his personal animal sphere and his spiritual being, is never overpowered by it; he is passive and submissive. The moral force of meekness and passive humility becomes a major factor in Dostoevsky's later theorizing, and its importance in his novels is evidenced by a series of characters, such as Sonya Marmeladov, Prince Myshkin, Sofya Andreevna Dolgoruky, Makar Dolgoruky, Alyosha Karamazov, and Father Zosima, who are endowed with these qualities. Though meek and submissive, they survive and conquer, and, as N. Gorodetzky puts it, "they prove to be the only ones who really exist." [1] They oppose self-assertion by self-denial, and violence by nonresistance. With them it becomes clear that true humility can be a powerful force. They are the real victors in life because they have no fear of suffering or personal humiliation. They have a firm bond with the earth from which they derive the power to accept and endure suffering without resistance, and in so doing they follow the path shown by Christ. Like Pralinsky and Golyadkin, they also suffer from their creaturely being, but they do not try to assert their selfish ego; they carry their burden humbly and without mutiny against their Creator. Unlike Dostoevsky's egocentric characters, they do not experience vindictive feelings toward those of their fellow men who are partly responsible for their own sin and suffering. Their humility imparts to them spiritual perfection at its highest level, for their attitude stems from their recognition of divine justice. In this way, they are profoundly important and meaningful in the scheme of creation. They accept unresistingly their earthly destiny as dual creatures, still finding it possible to live in accordance with the dictates of their spiritual being; thus they never deviate far from their true path in life. They are willing to undergo spiritual pain to atone for any sins they may have committed, convinced that in this they fulfill the will of God.

Sonya Marmeladov is one of these unselfish characters who sacrifices herself for others. In spite of her dismal destiny on this earth, she views the earth as sacred. Therefore she tells Raskolnikov, who is guilty of murder, that he has sinned against God and the earth: "Bow down," she advises him, "first kiss the ground which you defiled." Unlike Raskolnikov, she feels an inner bond with the earth and believes its laws to be the laws of God, upon which she would not presume to pass judgment; nor does she resist the evil in her life. Ever humble and meek, she accepts it as the suffering decreed to her by God Who can only be just and good. Although she does not know His intentions, she acknowledges His mystery: "What should I be without God?" she asks Raskolnikov, feeling that the will of God, Who ordained that man should suffer, embraces the whole world to which she also belongs. She feels she cannot exist without Him.

In a draft of *The Brothers Karamazov*, Dostoevsky writes, "*All is paradise*, but it is not given to many to see it." [2] Despite Sonya's anguish and sorrow, she feels this paradise; and this comprehension influences her in such a way that she becomes loving, forgiving, and instinctively wise. Truth is latent in her through a deep bond with earthly life, and through this bond she is also intimately connected with the "spiritual world." There is no need "to awaken a new human being" in herself. She believes that living for others is the only object of her life.

This experience of truth enables her to attain a higher reality through feeling, and without a preceding struggle with her reason, which, according to Dostoevsky, is never able to grasp such a truth. There is no need for her to be first sent out into the world—as Alyosha Karamazov is sent by Father Zosima—to take up the burden of suffering and through it grasp a higher truth. She attains it instinctively, for her original intuition, which is not impaired by selfish desires, enables her to approach moral perfection without a need to fight for it. The idea of morality is rooted in her so deeply that it is not possible for her to act contrary to the dictates of her conscience. Although Sonya's reason tells her that she is a "dishonorable creature," she acts against her logic and knows that it is her intuition—not her reason—which is right. This confidence is the guide which prevents her from taking a false step. Like Christ, Who assumed the burden of all human sins, she feels responsible for the sins of her fellow men. It is the fault of Sonya's stepmother that Sonya has become a prostitute; it is her father's sin that he does not interfere; and it is Raskolnikov's responsibility that she is exposed to spiritual pain. Yet she lives and suffers only for their sake.

Raskolnikov, who believes Sonya to be a person like himself, a criminal rejected by society, fails to notice that their offences are quite different. The motive for which he committed murder, if it existed in others, would lead the world to its death and destruction. He himself admits that he has killed the old woman for the sake of his "flesh and lust," without a thought of morality. The motive for Sonya's crime, on the contrary, could lead the world to its highest perfection if other people were guided in their actions by her attitude, which is similar to that of Christ. It is because of Sonya's advice that Raskolnikov decides to follow the path of suffering, and finally realizes the possibility of "a full resurrection to a new life, to a new and hitherto unknown future." He finds in himself, as Dmitry formulates it, "a new man," after he has accepted the way of pain and tribulation shown to him by Sonya.

Her power exists in her conviction that there is a higher reality above earthly reality. The tragedy of Raskolnikov is rooted in his inability to grasp this truth.

Like Sonya, Prince Myshkin also bears the torment and sin of those he loves. The blow in the face which he receives when he tries to prevent Ganya from hitting his sister is symbolic of the Prince's acceptance of responsibility for the sins of his fellows. Even Rogozhin's remark that Ganya would repent for having struck such a lamb as the Prince has a certain resemblance to the Biblical text.[3] Almost everybody present in the room is more or less guilty of Ganya's outrage; yet the blow is received by the one who is least guilty of any offence or unworthy impulse, the one who is merely trying to hold Ganya back.

The Idiot reveals the complexity of human guilt. It shows how the sin of one man brings about the sin of another, how the sin of one is dependent upon that of another, and how everyone is consequently responsible for the sins of the community. Society, in its rejection of Nastasya Filippovna, is concerned only with preserving the *comme il faut* ideals, with refined forms, which are the main object of the lives of the Epanchins, the Ivolgins, Totsky, and the others. "You all have a great admiration for the beauty and refinement of forms. That is all you care for. I have suspected for a long time that you care for nothing else," says Ippolit, mocking the family of General Epanchin. Had this society accepted Nastasya Filippovna, whose past does not quite correspond to the exigencies of "external beauty and propriety," these "beautiful forms" would have been destroyed. On the other hand, they are not tainted by Totsky who seduces a defenseless and unprotected young girl, imposes a burden upon her conscience, and exposes her to much contempt. The double guilt of society is seen in its tacit approval of her seduction and in her subsequent expulsion from social circles. Nastasya Filippovna, who is a victim of society but who also realizes only too well society's guilt, hates everybody and tries to avenge herself; the sin of the community brings about her sin. Her guilt-laden conscience not only has to cope with the sin of her moral fall, but also with her intense hatred. With little possibility of taking revenge on her fellow men, the only outlet for her vindictive passions is to remind them constantly of her degraded position. To attain this, she is frequently compelled to endure insult and humiliation, to make herself an object of public scorn. Finally, when she sees the impossibility of her return to the society to which she belongs by birth, she goes to Rogozhin knowing full well that death is awaiting her. The responsibility for her despair and death may be placed at the door of her fellow men.

Aglaya, in her longing to hurt the unfortunate Nastasya Filippovna, uses her own respected position in society. She vindicates her jealousy by intensifying her rival's spiritual agony. Rogozhin, filled with a blind passion for Nastasya Filippovna, seeks only his own gratification. In so doing, he sins against the Prince, tortures Nastasya Filippovna, and finally becomes a murderer.

At the end of the novel, Prince Myshkin, just as in the scene with Ganya, suffers for the sins of the others, who in their utter blindness, cannot recognize their common guilt. They are convinced that the break between the Prince and Aglaya is to be ascribed entirely to his failings. He loves Aglaya and pities Nastasya Filippovna, and when he must choose between the two he vacillates for a few seconds. Even that brief time is too long for the Epanchins who indignantly break off their relationship with him. "Oh, yes! I am guilty! Probably I am at fault all around! I do not quite know how, but I am at fault, no doubt!" moans the Prince, accepting the responsibility for all and everything. The others cannot see their guilt because they are unwilling to endure the suffering which may lead them to the truth, that same truth which gives Sonya Marmeladov the assurance that the hard way pursued by her is the right one decreed for her by a just and good God. Not prepared to bear pain, they never reach this goal and are left to depend on their "sound reason" with its *comme il faut* ideas and "beautiful outward forms." The Prince, on the other hand, like Sonya, is ready to face his destiny and can attain this truth, the highest reality.

The Prince lives in a world of reality unknown to his fellow men. Even Ganya remarks that Myshkin notices things and phenomena of which others are quite unaware. "You always observe what others pass by without noticing," Ganya states. The Prince inspires in the people about him a profound feeling of respect. Even while convinced that they listen to him merely for their amusement, they become attentive to his words and believe his judgment, for subconsciously they sense he is the best and the most worthy among them. Frequently unable to understand him, they cannot help but recognize his honesty, reliability, and innate wisdom. "I consider you the most honest and upright man," Aglaya remarks to the Prince, "more honest and upright than any other man; and if anybody says that your mind is . . . sometimes affected, it is unfair . . . your real mind is far better than all theirs put together. Such a mind as yours they have never dreamed of."

Most of the time, however, the Prince's fellow men laugh at him and do not take him seriously, since his concepts of love and of the inter-relationship between men differ so greatly from theirs. He appears to them a simpleton, another Don Quixote. They even consider him an idiot, just as Raskolnikov takes Sonya to be possessed by madness because of her constant sacrifices for her destitute family. The Prince, who is fully aware of this attitude toward himself, says to Evgeny Pavlovich, "There are certain great ideas, which I must not so much as approach, or I shall make you all laugh. . . . I have neither any sense of proportion nor of *beau geste*."

When Myshkin proposes to Nastasya Filippovna, people are bewildered by the line of his reasoning. "He is an educated but a lost man," General Epanchin says of him. Even Nastasya Filippovna herself is taken aback at his proposal and his insistence that she is "good and honorable." "Oh, these ideas come from novels," she replies to him, "they are merely old fairy tales. Times are changed now, dear Prince; the world sees things as they really are, and considers such ideas nonsensical." Yet the Prince still insists that she would confer an honor upon him by marrying him. "You have suffered," he says to her, "you have passed through hell and emerged pure, and that is much indeed." No one, not even Nastasya Filippovna, can understand this attitude, for everyone in the community is concerned only with facts and outward forms. Their motto is "love yourself before you love anything else." Ambition and vanity force them to cling to their "external beauty and propriety" in order that they may better conceal their natural condition with its base passions.

Among them, the Prince is the only one who is completely unselfish and who respects their personal interests. He has the ability to penetrate beneath external forms and events, and since everything he does and says is in agreement with his conception of morality, he is not disturbed by the mockery of the townsmen. These characteristics enable him to pursue the path toward self-abnegation.

In the final analysis, it is Rogozhin who is responsible for Prince Myshkin's insanity. Yet after Nastasya Filippovna's murder, which the Prince has tried in vain to prevent, he, now on the verge of mental derangement, gives the murderer the last thing he possesses, his brotherly love. He bears no grudge against Rogozhin and, together with him, guards the corpse of Nastasya Filippovna. Although he plays no part in her murder, he seems to share the murderer's guilt. The three people whom he loved most—Aglaya, Nastasya Filippovna, and Rogozhin—cannot rise above their selfishness. Engrossed only in their own selves, they are incapable of understanding and alleviating the suffering of others. They are not prepared to share the anguish and spiritual agony of their fellow men. In her surrender to Rogozhin, even Nastasya Filippovna herself does not seek suffering, but rather relief from it. Prince Myshkin, who endeavors to relieve them from their pain, accepts the full weight of their failings. Having loved them more than himself, he becomes a victim of their egocentricity. Like Christ, he has shown them the path of suffering, the way to attain the truth; and like Christ, he is held up to ridicule. His life is ruined by those whom he loved most and for whom he sacrificed all. "Prince Christ," as Dostoevsky refers to Myshkin in a draft of *The Idiot*,[4] is "crucified" by Aglaya and Nastasya Filippovna, who represent the egocentricity and selfishness of human nature.

We read in one of Dostoevsky's letters to A. N. Maykov, "When people read *The Idiot*, they will perhaps be somewhat astonished at its unexpected end. However, if they reflect about it a little, they will have to admit that this novel should have such an end. Indeed, I have succeeded in the ending, and only because of this ending."[5] To S. A. Ivanova, Dostoevsky reasserts, "To me, the fourth part and its ending are the most important things in my novel; that is, the whole novel has been conceived and written almost entirely for this denouement."[6] The idea which underlies *The Idiot* "is very good," he declares; "it is one of those ideas which do not take hold of you by their effect, but by their very essence."[7] It is important to consider Dostoevsky's own statements in the light of the novel's ending: Prince Myshkin is unable to change anything in the destiny of his fellow men; he can only show them the way to spiritual self-betterment, to self-abnegation, and to truth. They must make their own decision whether or not to follow this path. Inspired by Sonya Marmeladov, Raskolnikov finally finds in himself the spiritual force to accept suffering which leads to his moral rebirth. Prince Myshkin's fellow men fail to find this force and reject this solution. But it is shown clearly in the epilogue of *The Idiot* that Prince Myshkin is not forgotten. Like the memory of Christ, his also burns brightly in the minds of his fellows. The suffering he has borne is not futile, even though he cannot avert the tragic fate of the people he loves.

The artistic elaboration of this theme is found again in *The Brothers Karamazov*, when Father Zosima's mysterious visitor says to him, "We must keep the banner flying. Now and then, even if a man has to do it alone, he must set an example, and so draw the souls of others out of their solitude and spur them to some act of brotherly love, that the great idea may not die. He must do so even if in so doing he appears a fool to others." Prince Myshkin and Sonya Marmeladov, whose love prompts them to sacrifice themselves for others, are most important in the scheme of creation because they help, even if only involuntarily, to promote the striving of others for their ultimate goal. Though the people surrounding Prince Myshkin do not appreciate his suffering or acknowledge their own guilt, yet his acceptance of it for their sake remains "a beacon illuminating the path of others." Father Zosima expresses the same thought when he claims that "the righteous man departs, but his light remains." Even though people laugh at the Prince, it does not mean that his goodness is necessarily misplaced. Father Zosima, in his exhortations, says that even if an evil-doer "goes away untouched, mocking you, do not let this deter you. It shows his time has not yet come, but it will come in due course. And if it comes not, no matter; if not he, then another in his place will understand and suffer, and judge and condemn himself." Father Zosima believes the time will come when all men will accept their part in the responsibility for the world's crime and suffering, whereupon they will no longer sin. Therefore a "righteous man," such as Prince Myshkin, must not be discouraged if he appears to have failed in his aim. "Even though your light is shining," Father Zosima teaches, "and you see men are not being saved by it, hold firm and doubt not the power of the heavenly light. Believe that if they are not saved at once, they will be saved thereafter. And if they are not saved thereafter, then their sons will be saved, for your light will not die even when you are dead."

Primarily, Dostoevsky wanted the individual to perceive and become attracted by the "great idea" which animated both the lives of Christ and Dostoevsky's "meek" characters. Others, then, may be influenced by such a man.

This hope may be one of the reasons why Dostoevsky insists that he succeeded with the ending of *The Idiot*. In view of this optimistic note, some modern critics seem to have misinterpreted the spiritual idea underlying the novel. They also appear to have overlooked Dostoevsky's letters, a source which is far from esoteric. E. J. Simmons, for example, writes, "The conclusion of *The Idiot* leaves one with a painful sense of frustration. A powerful spiritual idea, magnificently developed throughout the novel, is refuted in the end by the evil forces of sinning men and women. . . . The futility of the spirit in its struggle against the sins of humanity seems poignantly symbolized in the sharp contrast between . . . Myshkin, arriving in St. Petersburg . . . and the final picture of him a year later." [8] One of the more recent critics, M. Krieger, voicing this rather traditional interpretation of the futility of Christian humility as incarnated by Prince Myshkin, demands that the Prince "must be rejected." And this for the following reason: Prince Myshkin's attitude does not improve his fellow men; on the contrary, "he gives them a greater moral burden than in their human weakness they can carry. They break under it and become worse than without Myshkin they would be." Thus "we are left with no further alternative possibilities," other than to retire, as did Prince Myshkin and Evgeny Pavlovich (for the latter "knows the futility of the problem too well to bother confronting it") in Mr. Krieger's interpretation. [9]

Such a pessimistic view hardly seems to be justified. Despite the tragic end of *The Idiot* (when the beautiful Nastasya Filippovna is murdered, the proud and impulsive Aglaya marries a Pole and becomes converted to Roman Catholicism, and the Christlike Prince Myshkin lapses into hopeless idiocy), the positive message of the book is not nullified, for the spirit of Prince Myshkin lives in the hearts of Evgeny Pavlovich, Vera Lebedev, and Lizaveta Prokofyevna. The Prince's failure in an intensely pragmatic world cannot be interpreted as negating the fundamental issue of *The Idiot* as a whole, for the idea of Christianity, which Myshkin personifies, remains as "a beacon illuminating the path of others."

It appears doubtful that Dostoevsky should be especially pleased with the ending of *The Idiot* and its underlying idea, if the refutation of this idea is actually implied by him at the end of the novel, as E. J. Simmons and M. Krieger see it.

The idea of the invaluable service rendered by the "meek" character in helping mankind to strive for moral self-perfection is further developed in *A Raw Youth*. Arkady Dolgoruky's mother, Sofya Andreevna, another character of the same unselfish type, accepts humbly and uncomplainingly everything fate sends her way. Like Sonya Marmeladov, she is not a person of great mind or learning, yet her natural wisdom surpasses that of a learned man. She does not resist evil in her personal life, but accepts it as something inevitable and ordained by God. She has no illusions, only "the fullest comprehension of her lot and the future awaiting her." She is afraid of everything that is new. Arkady thinks that "what matters to her is just that all is well and as it used to be; that there should be no change, that nothing new should happen, not even happiness." Sofya Andreevna's surprisingly passive nature reveals itself early when she consents to marry a man for whom she has no love, only a genuine feeling of reverence. "My mother looked upon her marriage with Makar Ivanovich as something settled long ago," Arkady writes in his memoirs, "and everything that happened to her in those days she considered very good and all for the best. She went to her wedding as unmoved as anyone could on such an occasion." [10] As the plot develops, she is seen accepting her life with the same passivity and meekness. Seduced by Versilov, she is grieved by the thought that she has succumbed to her "violent emotions," but does nothing to change her ambiguous position, and accepts her role in life as a sinner. Having started upon this path, she is determined not to evade responsibility for its consequences. Without complaint, she endures her hard life, with its frequent poverty, grief, solitude, and anguish. She is like the earth itself, all-enduring and all-sustaining. "Meekness, submissiveness, self-abasement, and at the same time firmness, strength, real strength, that is your mother's character," says Versilov to Arkady. "If I am afraid," Versilov asks Tatyana Pavlovna, "who will cure me of my terrors; where can I find an angel like Sonya?" Just as Sofya Andreevna remains natural throughout her life, so she remains constant in her feeling toward Versilov and finally becomes his loyal nurse.

Her courage to acknowledge and face the truth in everything imparts dignity to her being. She hates falsehood and refuses to accept Versilov's feigned affection. "You have given me charity, as if I did not know it," her flashing eyes say to Versilov, and she angrily disdains both his pity and charity. It is not accidental, therefore, that Versilov finds in her peace and spiritual comfort after his long, restless, and aimless wanderings in Russia and Europe. Throughout their life together, he has been aware that she will keep this peace ready for him. Her willingness to face truth and her strength to carry her cross—the strength which unites her with the earth and which results from her deep and intuitive understanding—help Versilov to find happiness and tranquillity. Once the outward world holds nothing further for him, he realizes his inability to attain his vague illusory ideals, and submits willingly to her wholesome influence and care.

Father Zosima, Sonya Marmeladov, Prince Myshkin, and Sofya Andreevna Dolgoruky, who have honestly admitted their guilt in the sins and sufferings of others, are sufficiently mature for paradise. Surprising as it may seem, old Marmeladov, Sonya's father, who appears to incarnate certain weaknesses of human nature carried to extremes, is also able to experience the Kingdom of God in his heart. Although perfectly aware that he is committing a crime against his family, he cannot find within himself enough strength to change the situation. In spite of these failings, he is sure that his sins will be forgiven because of the humility induced by the constant realization of his guilt. He freely admits his offenses in their entirety, and sees himself as the lowest of the low. With no courage to adhere to the truth, he is yet able, weak as he is, to expiate his guilt. He says to Raskolnikov, "And He will say, 'O, ye brutes! Ye who are made in the likeness of the Beast and bear his mask upon you, come ye unto me, too!' And the wise men will say, and the prudent men will say, 'Lord why dost Thou receive them?' And He will say unto them, 'I receive them, O wise men, I receive them, O prudent men, because not one of them thought himself worthy of it.' " [11] God will forgive Sonya's wretched father his sin against his family, for he continues to strive for moral perfection without hope of ever attaining it. According to Dostoevsky, a man who sins much, yet realizes the full depth of his sin, is better than a man who sins little without ever recognizing his own selfishness. Luzhin, Dunya Raskolnikov's fiancé, may be considered one of those "wise and prudent men" who, while disdaining Marmeladov's depravity, do not realize that morally they have sunk much lower.

Dostoevsky believes that man can attain moral perfection by daring to face the truth and by acknowledging his guilt, egocentricity, vanity and vice; man must also have the honesty to admit his impulse to control and dominate others, and his propensity to disregard their interests. The Underground Man, with his confession, and old Marmeladov, with his realization of the depth to which he has sunk, at least take their first step toward moral self-perfection. In Father Zosima's eyes, once a man has become entirely aware of his guilt, then the second step which leads him to his ultimate goal is boundless humility. Humility for Dostoevsky is many-sided: it comprises man's capacity to accept the destiny ordained by God, a willingness to suffer, his becoming sufficiently disinterested to shed his egocentricity, and his desire to serve God and humanity. If man has reached this stage, Father Zosima adds, his act of giving himself up to people and God shows his love for both; for love, according to Father Zosima, is nothing but a complete and boundless surrender of one's personality on behalf of others. This surrender, for Dostoevsky, recalls Christ. If all people follow in His footsteps and love their neighbors, then the law of God will prevail.

Dostoevsky firmly believes that eventually the time will come when people will love their fellow men as themselves. In this connection, he actually says,

> Why does man suffer even today and why is he unable to become a brother to others? This inability is reasonable, because brotherhood is the ideal of the ultimate form of human life, whereas man upon earth is merely in a transitory state. One day men will become brothers, but that will happen when man reaches his goal; then he will be transformed according to the laws of nature into a completely different being, who will neither solicit in marriage, nor indulge in unchastity. Moreover, Christ Himself preached that teaching as an ideal. He Himself predicted that until the end of the world there would be struggle and development (the teaching of the sword[12]), for this law is the law of nature. Life on earth is a process of development which in Heaven becomes complete, ever joyful and ever perfect. Therefore there will be no notion of time.[13]

This paradisaical life will come to pass only when each and everyone realizes his guilt and repents his sins, and thus ceases to blame his fellow men.

Dostoevsky's preoccupation with the problem of common guilt is clearly evinced in *The Brothers Karamazov*, as will be shown in the next chapter. Father Zosima maintains that "in reality each man is guilty before everyone else; only people do not realize this. . . . If they knew it, there would be immediate paradise on earth." If everyone tried to arrange life so as to prevent others from committing crimes and atrocities, perhaps there would be no crimes, argues Father Zosima. "If I had been righteous myself, perhaps there would have been no criminal standing before me," says he.

In "Stavrogin's Confession," Tikhon advises Stavrogin that honest people, after reading the latter's confession, will realize that the propensity to do evil is just as latent in them, but it is only a matter of circumstances that they have been spared from committing a similar crime. In "Stavrogin's Confession" as well as in *The Brothers Karamazov,* Dostoevsky emphasizes that were man to acknowledge his guilt in the sins of others he would advance considerably toward eternal harmony. The comprehension of man's guilt comes to him through bearing his cross. With the acceptance of this burden, he will be free from his impulse of self-assertion, and able to love his fellows. He will discern in them the likeness to God since they, too, will be devoid of their sins.

Dostoevsky's "meek" characters, passive and submissive as they may be, are effective agents in the transformation of man. This is mainly because of their inner strength to face the truth and acknowledge their guilt in the sins of other people. Since they are able to do this, they become those "righteous men," as Father Zosima calls them, who promote the aspiration of their fellow men for their ultimate goal. Prepared to serve and eager to sacrifice, they realize the unity of all creation and all creatures, and help to open the eyes of their neighbors to the purpose of their earthly existence.

IN DOSTOEVSKY'S WORKS the two opposing principles which
strive for dominance in the human soul are personified
in his characters. Sonya Marmeladov, Darya Pavlovna,
Prince Myshkin, and Father Zosima are the incarnation
of the principle which leads man to his chief goal. Humility, sacrifice and love are their marked characteristics.
Father Zosima teaches that it is only humble love and
self-abnegation which can change man to such a degree
that, wishing nothing for himself, he will live only for
the sake of his fellows, and thus convert life on earth into
a paradise. The opposite principle is embodied in Svidrigaylov, Stavrogin, Nastasya Filippovna, and Katerina
Ivanovna of *The Brothers Karamazov.* Concerned primarily with self-indulgence, they personify the principle
which prevents man from achieving his ultimate goal.

The novel in which this system of polarities is most
obvious is *A Raw Youth.* The two contrasting principles
are manifested here quite clearly: first in Arkady's
mother, whose life is based on self-sacrifice and humble
love; and secondly, in Versilov, who, despite his desire
for the harmonious unification of all ideas and nations,
has within himself inborn destructive tendencies.

In Versilov, Dostoevsky brings to light the primal elements of human nature from which ambition and man's
passions are compounded. Versilov is driven to spiritual
disintegration by the dual force within him. He plainly
recognizes the impulses responsible for his ambiguous behavior. He admits to Tatyana Pavlovna,

Do you know, I feel as though I were torn in two. . . .
Yes, I am really torn in two mentally, and I am horribly
afraid of it. It is just as though your second self were
standing beside you; one of the "selves" is sensible and
rational, but the other is impelled to do something perfectly senseless, and sometimes very funny; and suddenly
you notice that you are longing to do the same amusing
thing. Goodness knows why! This you want to do, as it
were, against your will. Though you fight against it with
all your might, you still want to.

When Makar Dolgoruky, on his deathbed, reminds
Versilov of his promise to marry Sofya Andreevna,
Versilov convinces himself that he intends to keep his
word, although his heart has already determined to leave
her and propose to Katerina Nikolaevna. Despite a feeling of moral obligation toward the mother of his children,
he is unable to suppress this passion for the other woman;
so fluctuating between these two contradictory feelings,
Versilov finally loses his mental equilibrium. As a result
of a fruitless attempt to consider his passionate desires
not as his own, Versilov is confronted by his double, who,
like Golyadkin's, comes to haunt him. Sometimes Versilov
even loses his dignity completely, as in the instance when
he begs Katerina Nikolaevna for charity.

The inclination toward evil for evil's sake, in Dostoevsky's eyes, is an ancient, basic force in man's being, a self-
evident variation of a fundamental metaphysical principle.
The novelist treats Versilov's moral tragedy, resulting
from the struggle between the principles of good and evil
within him, in the light of the spiritual tragedy of human
nature. Devoid of any bond with his homeland, Versilov
travels far and wide in Europe with no longing for the
country he has left behind. He can adapt himself easily to
life abroad: in France he is a Frenchman, in Germany a
German, in Greece a Greek; and as he becomes each, he
feels himself "most typically a Russian." He has certain
ideals, but even his perception of these is as nebulous
and indefinite as his feeling of nationality. Arkady's
former tutor describes him as "a nobleman of ancient
lineage," who "loves Russia, yet denies her absolutely."

"He is without any sort of religion, but almost ready to die for something indefinite, something to which he cannot give a name, but in which he fervently believes." During the period of seeking his abstruse ideals, he loses touch with the religion of his people, and thus unconsciously severs the last link with his motherland. He lives with a woman whom he loves, yet between them there is no mutual contact. He is a Russian nobleman, she is a peasant; and this difference in background, with all its ramifications, creates a deep cleavage between them, one which he is able to overcome only when he withdraws from social life. Prior to this, they had lived together in silence since their thoughts were so alien to each other's. Versilov himself tells Arkady that silence was the chief characteristic of their twenty-years' relationship.

The same silent alienation which he displays toward his *de facto* wife is characteristic of Versilov's attitude toward his fellow men. Isolated from them, he cannot believe in any real "love for humanity"; yet he does not see that this failure is his own fault. His attitude toward life is similar to that of the Grand Inquisitor: denying love, he has no faith in others, and views them as similarly unable to experience any unselfish feeling. His parental concern, therefore, impels him to warn Arkady, whom he thinks of as just another weakling, not to misuse the freedom of conscience which requires more inner strength from an individual than Versilov himself possesses. "One must keep a sense of proportion," he says to Arkady, "from now on you want to live a stormy life, set fire to something, smash something, rise above all Russia, call up storm clouds, throw everyone into terror and ecstasy, while you yourself vanish in North America. I have no doubt that you have something of the sort in your heart, and so I feel it necessary to warn you."

Arkady, although endowed with many of his father's qualities, is essentially different. He is resolved not to shrink from the suffering and burdens of life, and therefore, in spite of such weaknesses as vanity, pride, and self-indulgence, he is a stronger person than Versilov. He would have preferred a demanding father "like the ancient Horatio, who sent his sons to fight for the Roman ideal."

Arkady's childhood and youth were hard and solitary. At boarding school he had to suffer the humiliations imposed by his teacher and schoolmates. He was only a small boy when the stigma of his illegitimate birth was disclosed to him in a repulsive and cruel manner by his schoolfellows. He began early to feel the barrier separating him from others, and when he grew up he had an impulse to isolate himself from them completely. His desire to become a Rothschild was motivated by his longing to gain the self-confidence and self-reliance which he lacked in his early youth. Wishing to rise above others, he dreamed of power as a means of achieving the freedom of personality which he missed so much at school. But most of all he wished independence from society and its conventional ideas and notions.

Convinced that Versilov is mainly responsible for his spiritual trial, Arkady is at the same time ashamed of his own reproachful attitude since, in striving to become an independent being, he loathes making others responsible for his destiny. These two opposite feelings are characteristic of his nature. On the one hand, he is subject to a human tendency to make others responsible for his own suffering; on the other, his pride brings him to assume the responsibility for any blow which fate has dealt him. Considering a man who blames others for his suffering a coward, he continually struggles against this feeling in his own character. It is no easy task which he sets for himself, for there is no one to whom he can turn for guidance to achieve victory over himself. Versilov cannot show him the way because he himself knows so little about it.

The relationship between father and son constitutes an important aspect of the novel. Arkady earnestly tries to understand Versilov's nature and to assimilate some of his experiences. A significant issue in *A Raw Youth* is Arkady's genuine love and pity for his father. Although Versilov fails to give his son any spiritual support, the son comes to love him despite his weakness. Arkady neither judges nor blames him for his own trials, but rather loves his father more because of his involuntary sinning.

The two men have much in common. Like Versilov, Arkady at first strives to attain truth by logic and reason rather than by intuition. Realizing that he cannot be accepted by society because of his illegitimate birth, he is driven to a feeling of hatred toward the Russian nobility and, like Versilov himself, to isolation. Their fondness for comfort, their pronounced feeling of self-sufficiency, their adventurous spirit, even their passion for Katerina Nikolaevna, all are points of resemblance between them. But Arkady, by his perpetual courage to face facts and to strive for truth, succeeds in mastering his impulses. With constant care, he watches his own reactions; and, whenever he catches himself in a lie, he tries to retrace his train of thought and analyze for himself the motives behind the lie, be it deliberate or involuntary. This careful attitude grows as day by day he observes his father's shortcomings. They are constant reminders for him that he cannot rely on Versilov, but must make his own way in life.

When he witnesses an agonizing meeting between Versilov and Katerina Nikolaevna, Arkady is horrified by his father's self-abasement. "He had so far humiliated himself as to plead with her for charity! This depth of spiritual degradation was insufferable to watch!" he said to himself, but the instances of seeing his father's weakness are extremely valuable warnings to Arkady. When later in his own life he has a similar experience, he can recognize and face the truth about himself. He has a dream of Katerina Nikolaevna in which his covert desires are revealed to him. Although very ashamed, he courageously admits that these desires have been latent in him all the time. "It is because I have the soul of a spider," he admits; "it shows that all this has been lying dormant in my corrupt soul for a long time, and has been latent in my unconscious *desires*, but my waking heart was still ashamed, and my mind dared not consciously picture anything of the sort. In sleep my soul presented and laid bare all that was hidden in my heart, with the utmost accuracy, in a complete picture and prophetic form." Unlike his father, Arkady has sufficient moral strength to look at the truth squarely and acknowledge these abominable thoughts as his own.

This courage was characteristic of Arkady even in his early childhood. Once, while at school, he felt unable to endure humiliation and mockery any longer and planned to run away to his father. Just as he reached the point of carrying out his scheme, he suddenly abandoned it, recognizing in it his weakness and fear of reality. Later he told Tatyana Pavlovna, "A dark, dark night loomed black before me like a boundless, perilous, unknown land. . . . I stood, looked and slowly returned. . . . It was from this moment that I realized that I was a coward, and my real development began from that moment on." Having no parental control, he was often in trouble, even getting involved with a gang of blackmailers at one stage. That he did not succumb to the temptations put before him during his association with these people was due entirely to his ability to recognize the truth. In the same way, his fondness for comfort led him to become a gambler and a sponger for a time, but as soon as he became aware of the dangers connected with this tendency of his character, he again conquered the situation. This profound knowledge of his true nature and the courage to avow it are the factors supplying him with guidance throughout his life.

The full significance of Dostoevsky's concept of man becomes apparent in the person of Arkady. He embodies the following two principles: the principle of good, of striving for man's perfection, that is, the creative principle; and that of evil, the destructive principle. He is a symbol of man in general, the creature who loves to build and yet simultaneously destroy his edifice, in the words of the Underground Man, or a symbol of a force operating in two opposite directions, as Shatov formulates it. Only the elect, insists the Grand Inquisitor, have the inner strength to free themselves from the hindrances of the external world and achieve the ultimate goal of human existence. Arkady, in whom the principles of good and evil struggle with each other, cannot be classified as one of these elect; but he strives for spiritual perfection in spite of his inherited destructive impulses. This striving is made possible for him because, while aware of his dual nature, he is also aware of his ultimate goal, his moral self-betterment. Thus suffering, which the Grand Inquisitor considers a result of man's dual nature, has revealed its purpose and meaning through Arkady's subsequent striving for good. From his mother he learns the value of humble love, and from his father, the tragedy of the individual with destructive impulses. Arkady needs both of these revelations because, without them, he would not know what he struggles for or against, and there is no victory without a preceding struggle. From this viewpoint, A Raw Youth has great importance as a novel dealing with the development of the main character and revealing the dual nature of man.

The impression gained after reading the novel is that Arkady, despite the temptations and difficulties in his life, is on the correct path to moral self-betterment. It also seems that henceforth he will avoid the danger of isolation. Therefore, the burden of destiny imposed on him by his dual nature has found its purpose through his courage to face reality and to accept suffering. As his former tutor writes to him, Arkady has become "a new man" through this attitude. He has been bold enough to discard the mask of feigned virtues and well-simulated lofty intentions, and to see himself as he really is. Thus, he can confidently expect that the chaos caused by the feelings and thoughts of his early youth will eventually be resolved in order and harmony.

Man, Dostoevsky claims, in his striving for spiritual self-perfection, must not attempt to escape life. He must accept life with all its temptations and dangers, and make his way through them toward his spiritual goal. Like

Arkady, he must accumulate experience and learn from the failings of his fellow men, and his eyes must always be open to his own shortcomings.

ii

The problem of the acceptance of suffering finds its fullest artistic expression and philosophical significance in *The Brothers Karamazov*. As in *A Raw Youth*, in this novel Dostoevsky asserts that man comes to his goal, his spiritual self-perfection, not through pleasurable peace of mind, but by accepting suffering. This is an idea constantly preached by Father Zosima and expressed most clearly in the personal life of Alyosha Karamazov. He, although different in nature and in destiny, has one important point in common with Arkady Dolgoruky, namely their chaotic family relations, which are even more irregular in Alyosha's case than in Arkady's.

After living with remote relatives for many years, Alyosha returns home to see his mother's grave, and shortly thereafter enters a monastery. With this step Alyosha, who has experienced "the Karamazov thirst for the base life," is making a bid to escape the temptations of life. Dostoevsky is particularly explicit about the motive for Alosha's action when he points out that this decision is not dictated by fanaticism and mysticism, because Alyosha is "more of a realist than anyone." It is Alyosha's realism which suggests to him that the peace, silence, and seclusion of a monastery might provide an escape from the sensual instincts latent in the Karamazovs, and strengthen his soul in its search for self-perfection. "He entered upon this path," Dostoevsky relates, "only because, at that time, this idea . . . seemed to present an ideal means of escape for his soul from darkness to light." Alyosha's faith in God and immortality gives him the intensity and joy of living for them. "As soon as Alyosha reflected seriously, he was convinced of the existence of God and immortality, and naturally he immediately said to himself, 'I want to

live for immortality and I will accept no compromise.' "
With youthful confidence, he believes his goal will automatically be attained once he has sacrificed his pleasure-
seeking impulses. Since he has never really experienced
these earthly pleasures, nor given them the opportunity of
showing him their charms, he cannot be considered to
have triumphed over them. As in the case with Arkady
Dolgoruky, Dostoevsky, at this stage, again implies that a
victory is not possible without the previous struggle of at
least two opposing forces; that the surrender of feelings
and one's treasures, without awareness of their value and
the enjoyment they bring, cannot be considered a sacrifice.

In trying to evade temptations and suffering, Alyosha
misses the whole purpose of earthly life. Father Zosima,
sending him into the world, explains to him, "Life will
bring you many misfortunes, but you will find your happiness in them, and you will bless life." For the sake of
suffering Alyosha must leave the monastery. From his own
experience in life, he must come to realize that he is
guilty of the sins and suffering of others, as Father Zosima
advises him; he must understand and shoulder the responsibility for their failings, and finally become their teacher.

Dostoevsky's philosophy of suffering is a corollary of his
idea of common guilt. Man fails to live up to his better
self, and due to this failure moral guilt arises. As Prince
Valkovsky in *The Insulted and Injured* states, "There
is not a single man who is not a scoundrel somehow," and
who is not thus responsible for the shortcomings of his
fellow men. While in *The Idiot*, Dostoevsky only hints
at the guilt of society as a whole in Nastasya Filippovna's
murder and in Prince Myshkin's tragic insanity, in *The
Brothers Karamazov* he insists that every man is morally
guilty of the sins of others. This idea is developed in great
detail in the section entitled "The Recollections of Father
Zosima Before He Became a Monk." Father Zosima, who
in his old age attains a high level of spiritual and moral
perfection, has come to know through personal experience
how far egoism, egocentricity, and a fear of ridicule can

involve man in moral guilt toward his fellow men. Prompted by vanity, the young Zosima challenges an officer of his regiment to a duel, but later, recognizing his own excessive thought of self, decides he cannot burden his conscience with the death of another human being. He overcomes his vanity by refusing to fight the duel, an action which exposes him to the mockery of others. He not only agrees to bear this contempt but, to punish his pride further, asks his orderly for forgiveness, as one equal in birth and rank. However, vanity apparently still lingers in his soul, for that very day he arranges for the orderly's transfer to another regiment, to remove all memories of this incident.

Shortly thereafter, another event cures Zosima entirely of shame and pride. He comes to know a man of high social standing who murdered the woman he loved. Some years later, while happily married to another woman, this man is suddenly seized by a feeling of repentance, and a desire to make retribution by publicly confessing his crime. He is convinced that only in this way can he again find peace and happiness; but he still shrinks from making his confession, because his feeling of shame at appearing a criminal in the eyes of others is much stronger than the desire to do penance.

On hearing the story of Zosima's duel, this man gains new courage. He pays Zosima a visit and says with admiration, "You have dared to serve the truth, even when by so doing you risked incurring the contempt of all." Then he tells Zosima of the murder he has committed and of his intention to relieve his conscience of its insufferable torment by confessing his crime. Through this spiritual pain he has gained a deep insight into the human heart, and finally begins to understand that isolation is the basis of man's egocentricity and of his striving to benefit himself at the expense of his fellows. Zosima's example shows him the possibility of escaping this isolation, for Zosima knows the extent of man's guilt before all others: that in trying to assert his personality, man unconsciously inflicts suffering on them. When asked in a social gathering,

"How can man possibly be responsible for all?" Zosima replies, "Well, how could you understand it, since the world has long been going a different way, and since we consider obvious lies as truth and demand the same lies from others."

Dostoevsky expresses here a view that people are accustomed to think they are justified in living only for their own interests, without much consideration for others. They want to conceal from themselves the fact that each selfish action harms the whole community in some way or other. Therefore, to escape the pricks of conscience, they introduce conventions and social etiquette which enable them to cover their selfishness with notions of honor. The duel which Zosima will not fight is human vanity and egocentricity in the guise of moral obligation and honor. Dostoevsky further shows that the people who adhere to these notions will go so far as to expel from their circle those who fail to submit to these conventions, completely ostracizing people like Sonya Marmeladov and Nastasya Filippovna. They live in falseness and force others to do so also. Zosima, by his refusal to fight the duel, has struck one blow for the truth.

With this realization, Zosima's visitor also finds enough courage to face the truth and overcome the falsity of his life. He is looked up to as a respectable man of society, but in his own heart he knows himself as a murderer and a coward who is afraid to admit his crime. The hypocrisy behind his honorable reputation tortures him. Even now, when he is resolved to repent, he has no peace, only the constant fear that he will make his wife and children unhappy, and lose the respect of others. He cannot believe they will ever be able to esteem sufficiently his courage in avowing his guilt. "Will people recognize the truth, will they appreciate it, will they respect it?" he asks Zosima. Tormented and pained, he finally triumphs over his weakness and admits his guilt to the authorities. Now he "feels joy and peace for the first time after so many years."

Both Zosima and his visitor have exercised a mutually beneficial influence upon one another. Through his visitor's public confession, Zosima is assured that he himself has entered the right path in life. Man can attain "Heaven in his heart," he reflects, if he masters his selfish impulses. In so doing, he can succeed in becoming a spiritual and harmonious being. Zosima's visitor, triumphing over his animal self, "feels God near, and [his] heart rejoices as in Heaven." This experience of a fellow human being enables Zosima to conquer his remaining vanity and selfish desires. He knows now that this victory is possible only through fighting constantly against the animal aspect of human nature. He also knows that this fight is the inevitable result of the conflicting nature that has been implanted in man by his Creator. With this revelation Zosima enters the monastery in order to live only for his fellow men, to teach, and to help them in their spiritual distress. He has soared to the highest spiritual level and knows that man can attain this level only by suffering and acknowledging his guilt in the evil actions of all, in their corruption, anguish, and pain. "Accept suffering," Father Zosima preaches, "and bear it . . . and you will understand that you, too, are guilty."

Dostoevsky illustrates the idea of common guilt by showing that everybody in the town is responsible for the murder of old Karamazov. The evil which Fyodor Pavlovich's sin arouses in Dmitry and Ivan is turned against old Karamazov himself. Therefore, he shares with his sons the guilt of his own murder. Ivan and Dmitry hate their father because of his sensuality and greed, and most of all because they know they have inherited his base instincts and wild, passionate impulses. These impede their no less passionate striving for self-perfection.

Ivan wishes his father's death because of the old man's avarice. Though he has inherited his father's lustful nature, Ivan is unable to gratify his longings because Fyodor Pavlovich does not give him enough money. Dmitry, who is in love with Grushenka, hates old Karamazov mainly because of jealousy, and his ever-mounting antipathy is intensified by Fyodor Pavlovich's greed. Dmitry's greatest pain, however, comes from his vacillation between dual impulses. His "spiritual world" longs for self-perfection: "Glory to God in the world, glory to God in me," he recites to Alyosha. However, his spiritual side is debased by his wanton instincts. "Man is degraded," he complains; "there is a vast amount of suffering for man on earth, a great deal of trouble. . . . I hardly think of anything but degraded man. I think about him because I am that man myself." Realizing that man's spiritual side is his most valuable possession, and that his whole purpose in life should be to nurture this treasure, Dmitry longs to develop this side of his nature and discard the impulses which debase human dignity. He does not comprehend why man has been created with base instincts if he is intended for a higher purpose. "I go on and I do not know whether I am going to end in stench and disgrace, or in the attainment of joy and light. That is the trouble, for everything in the world is a riddle!" Dmitry complains to Alyosha, because he cannot understand why, as he strives to develop the spiritual aspect of his personality, he must fail even because of this striving.

Dmitry's betrothal to Katerina Ivanovna, who to him represents something ideal and elevated, is one of his attempts to develop his spiritual side. When the honor of Katerina Ivanovna's father is suddenly jeopardized by a mysterious deficit in his accounts, Dmitry, partly out of sheer bravado and partly out of his desire to avenge himself on Katerina Ivanovna for her inaccessibility and her contemptuous attitude toward him, offers to put forward the money if she satisfies his passion. With the full knowledge of what this visit means, she goes to him in order to save her father from disgrace. Dmitry, however, decides to be noble in spirit and, treating her as a lady, gives her the money and shows her out. In response, she bows down to his feet "in the Russian way, with her forehead to the floor." Dmitry is happy because his spiritual side has triumphed over his base inclinations. He is also delighted with Katerina Ivanovna for she appears to him now as an exalted noble being, endowed with genuine courage for self-sacrifice. He is convinced of her "lofty sentiments being as sincere as those of a heavenly angel." Even after the dissolution of their betrothal, when he knows the full extent of Katerina Ivanovna's vanity and self-love, Dmitry still regards their former relationship as the purest and loftiest recollection left to him.

Meanwhile he meets and becomes attracted to Grushenka, but because she is an "infernal woman," he thinks his love for her will "bring him into a dirty backalley . . . where he will sink into filth and stench." At this time Dmitry still owes Katerina Ivanovna money which she had previously entrusted him to send to Moscow as a test of his character. In love with Grushenka, he spends half of this money on her. Now he is torn two ways. He wants to return the money as soon as possible in order to prove to Katerina Ivanovna that he is not a scoundrel, but he also wishes to keep the money to spend on Grushenka should she come to him, as he hopes, and say, "Take me! I am yours forever!" The thought of using Katerina Ivanovna's money for this purpose and allowing her to witness his dishonesty sickens him. The two impulses—to return the money to its lawful owner, or to keep it for Grushenka—are set against each other within him with no hope of reconciliation. His striving to identify himself with his ideal, "God in the world," prompts him to follow the path to morality and subsequent self-betterment. His propensity for sensuality drives him toward the "vilest degradation," as he himself calls it. And always at the back of his mind is the thought that because of his father's greed he has no money; that had his father given him his due from his mother's estate, he would not now be in this terrible predicament. His participation in old Karamazov's murder arises from these two conflicting desires.

Dmitry's feeling of scorn and hatred toward Fyodor Pavlovich encourages, in its turn, Ivan's immoral desires. He hates Dmitry, and although he would not admit such a thought even to himself, he hopes his father will die by Dmitry's hand. Dostoevsky shows Ivan as subconsciously resolved to do as much as possible to encourage this state of affairs. Smerdyakov, too, hates Dmitry, envying his flamboyant way of life. Nor has Smerdyakov any love for Fyodor Pavlovich, suspecting him to be his natural father and so responsible for his low birth and unenviable position in life. Smerdyakov's greatest failing—which later compels him to commit suicide—is his inability to grasp both the ethical and unethical bases of Ivan's formula, "all things are lawful," by which Smerdyakov justifies his crime. This formula, Dostoevsky shows, comes not only from Ivan's concern and pity for his "feeble neighbor," that is, the spiritual aspect of Ivan's nature, but also from his creaturely being, which likewise gives rise to fondness for comfort and attempts to gratify his base passions. Smerdyakov, who fails to recognize these motives in Ivan's dual nature, is convinced that he has the right to murder Fyodor Pavlovich.

Even the kind and loving Alyosha, with his plans to serve only God, is in some measure guilty of his father's gruesome death; and his guilt, like Dmitry's and Ivan's, is also the result of his dual nature. Dostoevsky shows that Alyosha's love for God and his desire to know His goodness and justice are the main reasons for his succumbing to human weaknesses. He is conscious of the danger threatening the life of Fyodor Pavlovich. Father Zosima warns him to keep a watchful eye on his brothers lest crime and spiritual pain should enter their lives in the near future, but Alyosha is too engrossed in his own grief at the death of his beloved friend and spiritual father to heed this warning.

When Father Zosima dies, the monks and townspeople believe his body will not be subject to the natural law of decay. When Alyosha witnesses the first signs of decay in Father Zosima's body, he is heartbroken because he sees divine injustice in this decomposition. "Where is the hand of Providence?" he asks himself. "Why did Providence hide its face at the most critical moment, as though voluntarily submitting to the blind, inarticulate, pitiless laws of nature?" In grief, he suddenly feels an urge to follow in Ivan's footsteps and repudiate God's creation with its injustice, suffering and evil. In his heart there is only bitterness, and he has no wish to praise a creation in which the "sovereign of his heart" is denied a reward for his saintly deeds. Distressed at his disappointing experience of God, Alyosha completely forgets the dangers threatening his family. He is guilty of his father's death because in his preoccupation with the question of divine injustice and his great love and admiration for his teacher, he neglects everything else. As a protest against Providence, he yields to his Karamazov nature and visits Grushenka, of whose feminine charms he had always been afraid. This visit drives from his mind all thought of his brother Dmitry, who that very night goes to Fyodor Pavlovich's house. Later Smerdyakov tells Ivan that old Karamazov would not have been murdered if Dmitry had not happened to be there.

Dostoevsky shows that not only the three brothers Karamazov and Smerdyakov are to be blamed for the murder of old Karamazov, but also that Katerina Ivanovna and Grushenka are accessories to this murder in the same way as Nastasya Filippovna and Aglaya are responsible for driving Prince Myshkin to insanity in *The Idiot*. Dostoevsky portrays Katerina Ivanovna as being deeply hurt by the humiliation she suffers at Dmitry's hands. She can neither forget nor forgive him that she, a gentlewoman, was asked to sell herself for the price of her father's honor. "You used to visit gentlemen in the dusk for money once, bringing your beauty for sale," Grushenka maliciously points out to her, and this recollection fills Katerina Ivanovna with hatred. Dmitry's chivalry during her disgraceful visit deepens her misery, for she feels herself in a degree thankful to him. Because of these mixed feelings, she decides to equal his magnanimity by becoming betrothed to him: this is simply to repay his highmindedness and revel in her own virtue. By such a sacrifice she can see herself once more standing above Dmitry morally. "She is in love with her own virtue," Dmitry remarks bitterly in his conversation with Alyosha.

Dmitry's love for Grushenka wounds Katerina Ivanovna's vanity deeply because, once Dmitry does not need
her self-sacrifice, she can no longer believe in her virtue
and magnanimity. Still desperately clinging to the conviction of her own generosity, she determines to marry
Dmitry even at the expense of her love for Ivan. She
declares herself ready to forgive Dmitry's dissolute life
and his infidelity in love, and even to forego his love for
her. "I will become nothing but a means for his happiness," she decides, "or an instrument, a machine for his
happiness, and that for my whole life." "I will be a god to
whom he will pray." However, beneath her supposed
self-abnegation she hates Dmitry, for whom she feels she
must sacrifice her life and love of Ivan. Her spite grows
when he dares to prefer Grushenka to her, a beautiful,
refined, and wealthy lady of society. Dmitry, who is aware
of his fiancée's bitterness and disappointment, feels himself even more guilty, and his desire to return her money
grows stronger. Ivan, too, forced to stand by and watch
Katerina Ivanovna's humiliation, wishes more than ever
his father's death; he wants Dmitry to murder him, so
that Katerina Ivanovna will turn from her unfaithful
fiancé forever. Thus, the ideal of supposed noble highmindedness, toward which Katerina Ivanovna struggles,
makes her an involuntary accessory to Fyodor Pavlovich's murder.

Grushenka's guilt is of a similar nature. Seduced in
her early youth by a Pole, she was turned out by her
family and finally became the mistress of a rich old mer-
chant. Like Nastasya Filippovna, she wants to avenge herself on the world for her humiliating position in the
community. Using for this purpose Fyodor Pavlovich's
desire and Dmitry's love for her, she gives them both hope,
and kindles the flame of their passion, rousing their
hatred toward each other. When she becomes conscious of
her own love for Dmitry, the murder has already taken
place.

Dostoevsky further reveals that the whole community
is involved in this crime. All the people in the town are

equally at fault because of the covert human urge to do evil, an urge which their self-respect does not allow them to admit even to themselves. "You know," Liza Kokhlakov says to Alyosha, "it is as though people made an agreement to lie about it and have lied ever since. They all declare that they hate evil, but secretly they all love it." They know deep in their hearts that they only disguise their inclination toward evil. They may carry within them the ideal of spiritual self-perfection and strive for identification with this ideal, but because of their dishonesty with themselves, this noble ideal is reduced to a beautiful and hollow form. Most people, Dostoevsky considers, feel and act in the same way as Katerina Ivanovna, who wants to incarnate her ideal of magnanimity, but shrinks from acceptance of suffering which would lead her to her ultimate goal. They take no pains to become moral for they wish only to appear moral. Those who sink as low as Fyodor Pavlovich, Dostoevsky discloses, are often tempted to say, "Let me play the fool, for you, everyone of you, are more stupid and lower than I am." Like Miusov, who simulates moral indignation at old Karamazov's behavior, they are hypocrites and as remote from their moral ideal as Fyodor Pavlovich himself. They simply lie more often, and so can feign the observance of virtue—an effort which is of little interest to Karamazov.

Dostoevsky clearly indicates that the community is to be blamed also for Fyodor Pavlovich's distorted nature. The weaker a man is, and the more subservient to his creaturely being, the writer implies, the more strongly he comes to feel guilt in having betrayed his divine origin. The intensity of Fyodor Pavlovich's feeling of shame increases as he yields to vice and departs from his ideal of a good man. In an effort to conceal this shame even from himself, he seeks the respect of others in order to bolster his ego. When other people refuse him their respect, he tries to prove himself above their petty opinions through more flagrant displays of vice. The path toward his spiritual perfection becomes more and more obstructed by his dissolute and shameless life, and the real purpose of human existence is finally lost to him in a cloud of sin. Fyodor Pavlovich's hypocrisy springs mainly from the feeling of shame at his inability to identify himself with his ideal. Once having lost his self-respect, it becomes easy for him to hate his fellow men and despise their trivial opinions. Without respect, he sinks to bestiality in his vices. The attitude of the community is thus the seed from which springs the misfortune of the Karamazovs.

Fyodor Pavlovich's townsmen fail to follow Father Zosima's precept: "Brothers, have no fear of man's sins. Love a man in his sin, for that is the semblance of divine love and is the highest love on earth." In love for the sinner, man reveals his goodness and high morals. Genuine human love is a mark of spiritual perfection: it is love not only for the virtuous, but also for the sinful and debauched. Dostoevsky implies here that man should constantly aim toward this state. Fyodor Pavlovich is a weakling, and as such he can strive for his moral self-betterment only for the sake of a reward. As nobody helps him toward the path of goodness, he sinks lower and lower, and only in the presence of Alyosha does he feel himself a better man. "It is only with you I have good moments," he says to Alyosha, "you know that; otherwise I am an ill-natured man." Had the whole of society treated him in the same way as Alyosha, Dostoevsky implies, he would have become a good man, and the crime would not have taken place. His fellow men, however, in their striving for moral self-perfection, content themselves merely with beautiful and shallow forms; they even find secret pleasure in Karamazov's murder. They, too, seek the respect of others by feigning virtues—a precaution which Fyodor Pavlovich does not bother to take. Vain, selfish, and thinking only of their own well-being, they become isolated from one another and have neither compassion nor understanding for the failings of their fellow men. Some of them, like Ivan and Alyosha, by taking a false step, become responsible for the suffering or evil thoughts and intentions of others. Some others, like

Smerdyakov, envying the happiness of their more fortunate fellow men, desire only revenge because of their own dissatisfaction with life. Therefore, Dostoevsky insists, since human crimes are the responsibility of the whole community, every man must acknowledge his personal participation in the evil of all, and accept suffering.

Alyosha comes to understand common guilt after his father's death and, despite his own grief, finds enough strength to help others. This strength comes partly from Grushenka, whose innate goodness contributes to his moral victory. Alyosha goes to her as a protest against the injustice of God, but when he arrives and finds her in a state of despair, his frame of mind is completely changed. He understands that, although driven by the desire to take revenge upon society for her degraded position, Grushenka is closely bound to her native soil. She has always retained in her heart the faith of the Russian people, their notion of good and evil, and their predisposition to feel, think, and act accordingly. These spiritual and moral treasures prevent her from corrupting Alyosha, in whom she recognizes a pure youth. "Do you see how she has spared me?" Alyosha says to Rakitin, who took him to Grushenka with evil intent. "I came here to find a wicked soul. I felt drawn to evil because I was base and evil myself, and I found a true sister, I have found a treasure, a loving heart . . . Now she has saved me . . . Agrafyona Alexandrovna, I am speaking of you. You have raised my soul from the depths."

Just as Father Zosima and his visitor had felt, Alyosha and Grushenka are now aware that they have a wholesome effect on each other. With Alyosha's praises, Grushenka's conscience awakens and she realizes her own baseness: "Hush, Alyosha," she implores, "your words make me ashamed, for I am wicked, no good." She avows her evil intentions toward Fyodor Pavlovich and Dmitry, whom she has made fools of, and toward Alyosha, whom she had intended to seduce. This confession moves Alyosha's heart, and he, in turn, acknowledges his own shortcomings and sins. Thus, on the point of turning aside from the path leading to spiritual self-perfection, he becomes aware of his sin through another sinner; and through another's sincerity finds enough courage to be sincere himself. With this increased understanding of man's weakness, he now pities Grushenka with all her failings. "You must not ask too much of a human soul," he says to Rakitin, "you must be merciful." He believes in the intrinsic goodness of Grushenka's soul, though she is a sinner; and, in the presence of evil in his own heart, he realizes he must help his neighbors to find their goodness; he must be merciful toward them and love them even in their sin, as Father Zosima taught him to do. He must speak to them "not as a judge, but as the lowest of the judged," for no man is better than his fellow men: in each, inclination to do evil is equally latent.

Alyosha's and Grushenka's mutually beneficial influence and their subsequent understanding and love, which are great milestones on the way toward spiritual self-perfection, prove the wisdom of Father Zosima's message: Man must come to know life with its sins and pitfalls in order to become aware of the evil in himself. He must not turn away from evil without having been tempted to yield to its power, and must not seclude himself from the effects of human shortcomings. He must face these temptations courageously and, acknowledging base tendencies within himself, triumph over them, and so proceed toward his spiritual goal. Conscious of his sin and courageous and honest enough to admit it, he will not be deterred by the sins of others. With the realization that he is in some measure guilty of their failings, he will love and pity them. This attitude will enable him to grasp the real purpose of human life on earth. If man refuses to recognize his guilt in the sins of his fellows, he will lie to himself and come to hate them. With this hatred, human relations will deteriorate, as Dostoevsky shows in the scene involving Fyodor Pavlovich and Miusov. Conscious of Miusov's contemptuous attitude, Karamazov becomes defiant and impertinent, thus precipitating his own murder.

Man can be permitted to seclude himself from society for the sole purpose of serving God and immortality only when he has become aware of his own sin and can shoulder the responsibility for it. "Because we have come here," Father Zosima advises the monks, "and shut ourselves within these walls, we are not holier than those outside; on the contrary, by the very fact of coming here, each of us has confessed to himself that he is worse than others, worse than all men on earth. . . . Otherwise, he would have had no reason to come here." Thus, in order to realize his deficiencies and failings, man must not withdraw into solitude, but accept life.

As early as in 1849, while detained in the Peter and Paul fortress for his participation in the Petrashevsky circle, Dostoevsky expressed a similar thought with even greater conviction: "Life is everywhere, life is within ourselves, not in the external world. . . . To be and to remain forever *a human being*, neither to despair nor to fall in whatever unhappy situation one may find oneself, this is the meaning of life, this is its purpose. I have clearly realized this. This idea has penetrated my whole being." [1]

"Everyone should first of all love life," Alyosha explains to Ivan, who asks, "To love life more than the meaning of it?" Alyosha's answer is most significant in understanding Dostoevsky's philosophy of life: "Love life regardless of logic," Alyosha replies, for love of life, with its joy, pain, and struggle, is one step on the way to spiritual perfection.

iii

The Karamazovs may be taken as a symbol of mankind in their revelation of dual human nature. Through them we see man torn between his creaturely being, with its vanity, striving for comfort and accumulation of riches, and longing to dominate others; and his "spiritual world," the higher part of his personality, with moral perfection as its ultimate goal.

Dostoevsky ardently believes that there is a certain instinct to strive for moral self-betterment latent in every man, even if he indulges only in the gratification of his baser passions. There is no human being on earth, Dostoevsky maintains, who has not embodied within him the divine likeness, the image of Christ. Christ is a fundamental part of all men. "Even those who have renounced Christianity and attack it, have preserved in their heart the image of Christ, and have remained created in His image," Father Paisy advises Alyosha. Man, even if completely engrossed in himself and overwhelmed by his creaturely being, still has the consciousness of his "spiritual side."

Dostoevsky's conviction that positive qualities exist in every human being is particularly evident in the least sympathetic characters of *The Brothers Karamazov*. Greed, vanity, sensuality, and a longing to dominate others are characteristic of Fyodor Pavlovich, but the divine image has been preserved in his heart. He knows that as a human being he should live not only for the sake of self-indulgence, but also for the spirit. Dostoevsky calls him a nihilist who denies virtue, spiritual authority, morality, and God. In his heart, however, Fyodor Pavlovich is troubled with the question of whether God and immortality exist, and in his own fashion he is striving to find the truth. He admits frankly to Alyosha that he is only a blackguard, yet he is sincerely indignant with Smerdyakov, who believes that it is absurd to suffer for the sake of faith in God if there is to be no reward. A deep and serious meaning permeates old Karamazov's usually cynical words as he says, "Let me tell you, fool, that we are all of little faith because of our flippancy." This discussion with Smerdyakov throws him into a depressed state of mind, for he knows himself that on the whole his thoughts resemble those of Smerdyakov.

Aware of the contempt in which he is held, Fyodor Pavlovich feels he cannot start a new moral life; he has no desire to become a "most amiable and wise man" because his fellow men will not give him the respect which he considers his due. Only Alyosha understands that his father's "heart is better than his mind," since it is the heart which reveals to Fyodor Pavlovich that real virtue is a result of man's innermost knowledge of good and evil, and does not demand a reward. "You try to be virtuous in life, to do good in society, without being confined to the monastery, receiving your bread free, and without expecting a reward in heaven; you will find that a bit harder." "Why do you expect a reward in heaven?" Fyodor Pavlovich sarcastically asks the monks. His inner conviction that real virtue does not presuppose recompense proves that even a complete libertine is potentially capable of striving for moral self-betterment. He only appears to have lost his connection with God, for the roots of the divine image are also alive in him, as in any other human being, however deeply they may be buried beneath his sin and depravity. Even if his "spiritual side" lies dormant, he has self-knowledge and is aware of his own worthlessness. He does not even try to cover up his baseness with a pretense of virtue, and while assuming moral indignation at Dmitry's behavior during their visit to the monastery, he confesses to himself, "You know you are lying, you shameless old sinner! You are shamming now, in spite of your 'holy' wrath!" His hypocrisy springs from a feeling of shame at his inability to identify himself with his ideal.

This courage to be honest with himself is also characteristic of Smerdyakov, who is described by Dmitry's defense counsel as a malicious, revengeful, wicked, and envious man. At the root of Smerdyakov's crime is his belief in Ivan's formula that "all things are lawful," and therefore he feels justified in taking the initiative to determine his own fate. Convinced as he is that the life decreed to him by God is unjust, he is resolved to murder Fyodor Pavlovich, whom he holds responsible for his misfortune and misery. He even feels that in stealing the old man's money he is merely making amends for the injustice that has beset his life. Later, however, he realizes that he has murdered Fyodor Pavlovich under a false premise and this cuts the ground from beneath his feet. It appears senseless to him to lie now, because if he did, he would have to persist in the conviction that "all things are lawful," a creed which he no longer believes. Though too weak to accept suffering and confess to the authorities, he refuses to live a life of falsity, so his only way out is suicide. Self-destruction is his way of giving truth its due.

Since every man is made in the image of God, the striving for spiritual self-perfection remains his secret ideal, however much he may succumb to vice and depravity. "Who does not go astray at least once in his life?" the Ridiculous Man inquires. "Yet we all, from the sage to the lowest robber, strive for the same goal!" This striving is pronounced in the brothers Karamazov. They yearn for faith in divine justice, but Dostoevsky makes them first go through the purgatory of tormenting disbelief. Ivan, who desires to solve the problem of immortality and the justice of God in the affirmative, must first deny it in order to experience a longing to give "a quadrillion quadrillions for two seconds of joy." Alyosha warns Ivan that he will not be able to endure his guilty conscience if he should deny Christ, but Ivan maintains that there is a strength in him to endure everything, and that is "the strength of the Karamazovs . . . the strength of the Karamazov baseness." Because of this baseness, Ivan's struggle for God and immortality is painful, but the harder the fight, the greater the triumph of victory. For the sake of this victory over himself, Father Zosima prevents Alyosha from retiring into the monastery, but in the novel, it is Ivan, not Alyosha, who is subject to the greatest torments in his fight for moral victory.

It is significant that, although Ivan finally becomes insane, while ready to take up suffering and endure the hell of unbelief, Dostoevsky hints at his regeneration. When Alyosha informs Dmitry of Ivan's mental illness, Dmitry replies, "Our brother Ivan will surpass everyone. He ought to live, not us. He will recover." Similar allusions are found in Dostoevsky's notes: "Dmitry, smiling good-naturedly about his brother Ivan, says, 'He has failed to endure his torture (but he will endure it. He will surpass everyone. He is not such a person as I!)'" [2] "Dmitry utters mysteriously about Ivan, 'He is a real man . . . He is a superior man. He is not like you or me.'" [3]

Ivan, with his powerful intellect and the tragic intensity of his struggle, undoubtedly belongs to those whom the Grand Inquisitor calls the "elect." Though strong enough to shoulder the responsibility of his conscience, Ivan raises his "free banner" against Christ because he is unable to justify the apparently senseless misery of human existence; yet his ardent desire to give up everything for two seconds of joy leaves the door open for the possibility of his ultimate triumph over the negative side of his nature. His hosanna "must be forged in the crucible of doubt."

This feature of Ivan is much misunderstood. Even a critic as sensitive as Romano Guardini considers Ivan merely a miserable weakling, and his Grand Inquisitor a ridiculous parody of Ivan's superman. "Ivan has acted 'the Grand Inquisitor,' the superman," Guardini writes, "but what a miserable superman! His actions are just as petty and helplessly inconsistent as those of Raskolnikov. He is slipping to his doom." If the Grand Inquisitor were honest with himself, he would have admitted, like Raskolnikov, "Yet I am no Napoleon! I am only a louse!" [4]

This appears to be an unjust criticism. The Grand Inquisitor admits involuntarily furthering Satan's aims, but he shoulders the whole burden of human suffering and responsibility. "Isn't it suffering, at least for a man like that, who has wasted his whole life in the desert to perform a great deed, and yet could not shake off his incurable love for humanity?" Ivan asks Alyosha. The Grand Inquisitor is fully aware that, while he tries to make man's earthly life comfortable, without suffering, he is deceiving his beloved humanity and leading it to inevitable ruin. He, thus, belongs to the martyrs, who, as Ivan expresses it, "loving humanity, are oppressed by great sorrow." It seems, therefore, unjust to explain the

Grand Inquisitor's actions and his profound love for humanity as being attributes of "a petty louse." He is not a weakling, at least not to Dostoevsky. Ivan, then, who seeks and accepts suffering, must also be anything but a weakling.

Guardini further maintains that Ivan's denial of God lacks entirely the intensity of Kirillov's. This viewpoint is not in accord with Dostoevsky's own interpretation of Ivan's attitude, for he writes with reference to Ivan's atheism, "Even in Europe there has never been atheistic expression of such power. Consequently, I believe in Christ and profess myself a Christian, but not as a child; my hosanna has been formed in a great furnace of doubt, as the devil puts it in my last novel." [5]

As with Ivan, Dmitry's striving for spiritual perfection is also strong. The idea that the individual must share the guilt and suffering of others is finally perceived by Dmitry, just as it is by Father Zosima, who bows down before him as one condemned to suffer. This perception comes in a dream which reveals convincingly that people through their sins are guilty of the suffering of their fellow men, and that because of this, even innocent children must suffer. Dmitry, who now yearns to participate in the atonement of universal human guilt, is ready to accept joyfully the punishment for his father's murder. Aware that his spiritual pain can lead him to moral self-perfection, he anticipates his punishment with rapture and exultation. He now knows that through his anguish he can be reborn, that his suffering can guide him to a beatific faith in God and immortality. But, despite this revelation, Dmitry realizes that his spiritual strength will not suffice for him to bear his cross. His state of rapture is short lived, because he does not know humility, which is one of the most significant prerequisites for enduring suffering; he cannot even suffer humbly the scornful attitude of the jailers. Since he is not ready, like his brother Ivan, to give "a quadrillion quadrillions for two seconds of joy," he does not belong to the category of the "elect." Realizing that Ivan is a stronger and greater man, and having become mature through his present awareness of the meaning of suffering, Dmitry says to Alyosha without the slightest trace of envy, "Ivan ought to live, not us."

Dostoevsky shows that even Alyosha, with his willingness to suffer, is not one of the elect like Ivan. Although Father Zosima advises him to experience life with its pain and sorrow, it is apparent that Ivan's intense struggle has not been granted to Alyosha. A firm faith in God and immortality becomes his lot almost without spiritual pain; therefore his life is, like that of Dmitry, less tormenting than Ivan's, although both Dmitry and Alyosha have come to know that the true meaning and purpose of life lies in suffering. Through his personal experience, Alyosha has become an understanding man, ready to extend a helping hand to those in spiritual distress. He realizes that Dmitry is not born to endure the pain of life, so he warmly consoles him by saying that the comprehension of the meaning and value of suffering must suffice him in striving for man's goal. "You are not ready, and such a cross is not for you. What is more, you do not need such a martyr's cross since you are not ready," he counsels Dmitry. "You wanted through suffering to revive in yourself another man. I think you must only remember this other man always, all your life and wherever you go; and that will be enough for you."

Though these are the words of a wise man who understands and allows for human sins and imperfections, they may appear somewhat misleading. Alyosha's opinion that Dmitry is not born for trial and affliction is consistent with the latter's character, but these comforting words may encourage his natural impulses. According to Dostoevsky, however, since the two brothers have now seen the truth that suffering is the meaning and purpose of life, in the future they will follow more closely the path leading to the consummation of their spiritual lives. Even if sometimes they yield to their baser passions, they will not stray far from their righteous course. They both can see what the Ridiculous Man saw when he said, "Of course, I shall go astray often . . . for who does not make mistakes? . . . But I cannot go far wrong, for I have seen the truth."

All depends on this truth, Dostoevsky insists, on man's ideal of spiritual perfection, which must shine before him as a beacon through the mist of errors and blunders. If he neither forgets nor renounces his ideal, but beholds it all his life long, he will ultimately attain the truth, and will fulfill the purpose preordained for man upon earth. If man loves every living thing in the world, as Father Zosima teaches, this love will justify suffering, and all will share each other's guilt. This is Dostoevsky's final message. For him, there is only one way to this truth; the way of the Karamazovs, who symbolize the whole of mankind.

Self-knowledge, which is the most essential ingredient in reaching this goal, is attainable only by living man's chaotic and tragic life and experiencing its constituent parts, joy and suffering, light and darkness—the life lived by the Karamazovs. To follow this path, man must be endowed with the dual qualities underlying God's entire creation. Just as the "X" is required for an equation with one unknown, so also is the negative, destructive principle —"the indispensable minus"—necessary for the preservation of earthly existence. Consequently, man's creaturely being must be given its due. Man must retain both his spiritual world and his natural self; he must be able "to contemplate simultaneously two infinities: the heights above him, the heights of loftiest ideals; and the depths below him, the abyss of the vilest and most fetid degradation." These contradictions in human nature, which cause man's suffering and his struggle for the consciousness of reality, enable him to strive for his spiritual self-perfection, leading him ultimately to the region of the absolute, and to eternity.

9 CONCLUSION

THIS STUDY has been an attempt to trace the reflection of Dostoevsky's dualistic outlook in his fiction. An attempt has also been made to analyze those manifestations of human duality which form the basis of his novels. His writings emanate from and embody his fertile and complex spiritual experience, often revealing his artistic propensity to illuminate a problem from various viewpoints. He does not merely offer a series of hypotheses, but struggles with himself in an effort to reconcile logical thought with intuitive vision. This interplay of ideas is best seen in two areas of his thought: first, the possibility of a paradise on earth, and second, the significance of man's reason in life. In the person of Ivan Karamazov, Dostoevsky shows that although reason is the basis of man's duality, Ivan's intellect still is highly praised by Father Zosima because it is this faculty which enables Ivan to contemplate lofty ideals and ponder spiritual problems. His reason brings him much suffering; but suffering, for Dostoevsky, is a prerequisite for the fullest development of man's awareness of reality.

Dostoevsky admits that man's ideal existence is only a beautiful dream; that earthly life in its present form results from the duality of the universe; and that an ideal world order can bring only stagnation and death. Such conclusions, however, are alien to Dostoevsky's intuitive perception, and thus he continues to yearn for an ideal life on earth. This leads him to postulate that man's reason alone cannot establish principles by which all men can live in universal peace and happiness. He decides that if man abandons reason as a guiding factor in life and relies on intuition, he will be closer to an existence which is based on the love and goodness that dwell in the hearts of all people. Man's spiritual being will conquer his animal self, and he will live in harmony with others. Both his struggle for existence and his knowledge of evil will be relegated to the past, for his natural self, now free of egoistic impulses, will be emancipated from its evil nature.

In spite of this polyphony of unresolved ideas,[1] Dostoevsky's fiction as a whole reveals a unique consistency. N. Berdyaev, when speaking of Dostoevsky's vision of the world, comes to the following conclusion: "If Dostoevsky had completed his theory of God, of the Absolute, he would have been forced to recognize the polarity of divine nature itself." [2]

The theme of duality, as it appears in Dostoevsky's works, is not new. Throughout the ages, man has confronted one of the most complex and still unsolved problems, that of the nature and origin of evil. Unable to reconcile the concept of good, justice, and absolute morality which he attributes to God with the obvious limitations of the world of objective reality, man, as Dostoevsky sees it, begins to doubt the existence of God. He is at a loss to explain with his intellect the relationship between the perfection of God and the imperfection of His creation; between the absolute and the contingent; between the infinite and finite. A witness to man's moral and physical misery in the enveloping world, he attempts to determine its origin and cause. Behind some of the solutions offered, there is an attitude which could be termed dualistic.

The origin of systematic dualism can be traced to Gnosticism and was later amplified into a classical formulation by Manichaeism. Mani's teaching places the problem of evil in the foreground and develops the theory of two substances, light and darkness, which are the cause of the struggle between good and evil in the soul of man and in the world surrounding him. The basis of this theory is a fundamental opposition between good and evil: light is the source of good—it is the origin of the pure and beautiful, the principle of order and harmony; darkness is the cause of evil—it is the origin of the impure and painful, the principle of division and discord. The world has originated from the constant struggle between these two principles. Matter, dark and multiple, is responsible for the origin of evil, and as such, is radically opposed to the spirituality and harmonious unity of God. Man reflects this cosmological dualism in a microcosmic form; his spirit is of divine origin, whereas his body is irredeemably evil. Through the body, the powers of evil seek to impair the light and beauty of the soul, to confine it in the darkness of matter, and to sever its relationship with the heavenly spheres. Evil does not result from the abuse of man's free will, but is inherent in his physical body, and is thus rooted in life itself. Manichaeism further teaches that, although man is absolved from any responsibility for the existence of evil in the world, he must strive through his deeds for the purification of his soul from the contagious influence of its material garment. These essential tenets of Manichaeism, more recently revived in the doctrines of John Stuart Mill, Wilfred Monod, and Émile Lasbax, might have exerted some effect upon Dostoevsky's views.

Dostoevsky's concept of man also has a strong resemblance to the Zoroastrian teaching on human nature, with its stress on the importance of man's body and free will. Zoroastrianism, which holds that suffering lies in the very nature of man as a free being so long as he remains in his present form, played an important part in the ideological development of European thought and religion long before the time of Dostoevsky. Similarly to Zoroaster, Dostoevsky maintains that the purpose of human effort is not to abolish suffering, but to understand its meaning as proof of divine justice, for only those who are not afraid of pain are mature and truly free people. Considering suffering as an absolutely necessary element in achieving universal harmony and bliss, he emphasizes its significance to an extent hitherto unknown in Russian literature. He believes that when mankind reaches its ideal order, the present suffering of the innocent will to justified through the love of God which reveals itself in Creation through Christ.

Implicit in Dostoevsky's work is the following sequence of thought: God is the creative spirit, the love out of which He created the world. Without Creation, God would not be God. He would be at most a cold light, shining in the midst of a huge solitude. He could not be that living, glowing flame which creates out of itself a multitude of beings; the flame which impels all beings to partake of its glory. Man's spirit enables him to strive for the perfection of his Creator, for in this is the consummation of God's Creation. If this instinct to strive were not imparted to man, life would represent an incessant cycle by which everything that dies is reborn; life then would be an end in itself, without any further meaning or purpose, the logical development of Schopenhauer's philosophy. Unlike Schopenhauer, Dostoevsky believes that life is a process of development which will be completed at some unknown time. Therefore, the suffering which ensues from man's destiny of being simultaneously spirit and matter is justifiable.

For Dostoevsky, suffering is not only the natural outcome of man's duality, but also gives meaning to this duality. The literary development of this theme leads him to the conclusion that in order to bring God's Creation to its triumphant perfection, man must attain the creative spirit—the all-embracing love—by means of which Creation came into existence. Dostoevsky makes his wise Father Zosima express his final and highest perception in the following words: "Loving submissiveness and humility are marvellously strong, the strongest thing of all, and there is nothing to compare with them." He classifies this love as humble and submissive, because it is an all-encompassing love; a love for the whole Creation, with the painful polarity of its forces. It is a love which embraces the most insignificant creatures of God, a love which is complete self-abnegation. If Creation can give back in full measure the love out of which it was born, then it achieves its highest perfection. Man alone is able to experience this great love, since only in him are united the two constituents of divine Creation, matter and the creative spirit. Man suffers because of the incessant struggle between his spiritual world and his animal being: he denies his natural self for the sake of the spirit; but at the same time, in order to exist as an earthly being, he must also deny his spirit to satisfy his instinct of self-preservation. Suffering, springing from and yet uniting within itself the two opposing forces of Creation, matter and spirit, is the highest form of man's consciousness of reality. Dostoevsky considers this consciousness to be the only means for the affirmation and acceptance of Creation.

From an analysis of Dostoevsky's views it becomes evident that in suffering lies the highest significance of Creation, since Creation can affirm itself only through the spiritual pain experienced by man, and the full reciprocation of the Creator's love. In this way Creation can reach its consummation. As Father Zosima writes in his exhortations, "The Creator, just as in the first days of creation He ended each day with praise, 'That which I have created is good,' looks upon Job and again praises His creation. And Job, praising the Lord, serves not only Him but all His Creation." Therefore, for Dostoevsky, the reason for Christ's refusal to descend from the cross was His desire to fulfill His suffering by voluntary surrender to the causal laws of nature, to give all for the sake of highest perfection. This surrender was made possible through the strength of His humble and submissive love, in the name of the acceptance of God's Creation. Christ, by this acceptance, showed mankind the pathway leading to perfection, and answered, once and for all, the question of whether the suffering of the innocent is justifiable. Christ, the expression of divine justice, voluntarily shed His blood for all. With this knowledge, Dostoevsky has found the meaning of duality and its natural consequence, which is suffering.

Just as the struggle between matter and spirit brings Creation to its perfection through man's suffering, so, in Dostoevsky's opinion, the struggle between good and evil is similarly necessary for this process. Dostoevsky portrays the struggle of these two principles most forcefully in the figures of Christ and the Grand Inquisitor in "The Legend of the Grand Inquisitor." Christ's kiss may be taken as a symbol of the unification of good and evil in suffering. The opposing aspects of man's nature, his spiritual capacities and animal being, are similarly united. Dostoevsky emphasizes that only in man are these polarities brought together, and only for man does this tormenting duality exist.

Dualism, as a concept of the world, existed long before Dostoevsky, not only in abstract philosophical doctrines, but also in fiction. Reference to man's inward dualism goes far back into ancient times, and its origin can be traced to primitive religious and ethical beliefs, with their juxtaposition of good and evil in allegorical presentation. In literary tradition, this allegorical treatment of man's dual nature assumed the form of the *Doppelgänger*, who embodies the element of evil in man. In the writings of H. v. Kleist and Z. Werner, the conflict between the opposing aspects of the personality and its subsequent disintegration into two discordant and even irreconcilable entities, is reflected in the "love-hate" motif. The works of E. T. A. Hoffmann, A. v. Chamisso, and Wilhelm Hauff also portray the dissociation of the personality and elaborate the various forms in which the unconscious self manifests itself to the subject's normal self in his waking hours. The themes of duality reappear in the writings of Edgar Allan Poe, R. L. Stevenson, and G. de Maupassant.

While Dostoevsky did not invent the dual personality, his treatment of the traditional theme of duality is strikingly original. He does not indulge in scenes involving somnambulism, magnetic abstractions of mind and spirit, maniacal junctures, and supernaturalism—the characteristics which diminish the realism of the German romanticists. He also excludes the malign "gas-lit" specters of post-romantic fiction—the devices of Poe, Stevenson, and de Maupassant. His portrayal of the *Doppelgänger*, furthermore, has little in common with either Hoffmann's world of fantasy, with its horror of natural phenomena, or with the grotesquely absurd situations of Gogol's presentation of the double in "The Nose."

In Dostoevsky's novels, the whole emphasis is placed on the analysis of the irrational regions of the human soul. His intense concentration on the inner world of his heroes distinguishes him from practically every other Russian writer. In a letter to his brother Mikhail, he himself characterizes his method in a way which can scarcely be bettered: "They find in me a new and original spirit, . . . in that I proceed by analysis and not by synthesis, i.e., I plunge into the depths and, while I dissect the whole into atoms, I bring out the whole." [3]

This new approach puts the impress of a powerful individuality on his works, and opens up new literary vistas. To express man's duality, Dostoevsky uses a special technique of dialogue and develops such artistic devices as dream logic, dreams, hallucinations, and symbols to a degree previously unknown. All this bears witness to his originality not only as a psychological novelist, whose fiction "found its deepest inspiration in the 'philosophy of the human spirit,'" [4] but also as an artist. Dostoevsky's greatness lies also in his ability to extract the "essence of the real," and in his exhaustive exposition of this essence. Without destroying probability, he goes beyond what is empirically definable, and shows the depths of man's conscious and subconscious existence. His steady concentration upon what is universally and basically human reveals an intellectual and spiritual complexity which is the essential characteristic of modern self-awareness. Probing into the mind of man, the novelist reveals hitherto unsuspected entanglements of human psychology. The characters thus analyzed are then exposed to all the complications of modern society. The greatest of his discoveries is that man cannot be explained in purely human terms; that in him is contained the secret of the whole universe, and that in him is concealed its final revelation.

As the problems raised in Dostoevsky's novels reflect conflicting issues which have no relation to time or space, his hypnotic art, with its dreams and hallucinations, its far-reaching insights and metaphysical truths, its pathos of belief and agony of doubt, has become universal. As such, it remains unparalleled in world literature. Dostoevsky, an extraordinary observer of the irrational in man, a profound analyst of subconscious urges and complexes, and an intuitive explorer and seer of remote metaphysical depths, speaks to his reader, in the words of Thomas Mann, "in the name of and out of love for humanity: on behalf of a new, deeper and unrhetorical humanity that has passed through all the hells of suffering and understanding." In André Suarès's happy formulation, Dostoevsky has "the greatest heart, the deepest consciousness in our modern world."

Dostoevsky indeed introduces his reader to a deeper psychological understanding of man in general and reveals the fundamental principle of all-forgiving and all-embracing love. Through his revelations, man can be understood more fully.

Introduction

1. D. S. Merezhkovsky, *Vechnye sputniki* (St. Petersberg: Wolf, 1911), p. 212.
2. A. Schopenhauer, *Die Welt als Wille und Vorstellung*, 2 vols. (Leipzig: Hesse & Becker, 1919), I, 523.
3. *Ibid.*, I, 499.
4. As Dostoevsky puts it, "with the instinct for self-preservation in the foreground." See *Zapisnye tetradi F. M. Dostoevskogo*, prepared for publication by E. N. Konshina, commentaries by N. I. Ignatova and E. N. Konshina (Moscow-Leningrad: Academia, 1935), p. 211.

1—Duality as Spiritual Background

1. F. M. Dostoevsky, *Dnevnik pisatelya za 1876 god* (Paris: YMCA-Press, n.d.), p. 472.
2. Ref. Dostoevsky's letter to M. N. Katkov dated September, 1865, in *Dostoevsky—Pisma 1832–1867*, ed. and annotated by A. S. Dolinin (Moscow-Leningrad: Gos. Izdat., 1928), I, 418.
3. *F. M. Dostoevsky—Materialy i issledovaniya*, ed. A. S. Dolinin (Leningrad: Izdat. Akademii Nauk SSSR, 1935), p. 156.
4. N. Berdyaev, *Spirit and Reality* (London: Geoffrey Bless, 1936), p. 23.
5. *Dostoevsky—Pisma 1878–1881*, ed. and annotated by A. S. Dolinin (Moscow: GIKhL, 1959), IV, 5 (letter to L. N. Ozmidov dated February, 1878).
6. N. Berdyaev, *Freedom and the Spirit* (London: Geoffrey Bless, 1935), p. 27.

7. Ref. J. G. Davies, *The Theology of William Blake* (Oxford: Clarendon Press, 1948), pp. 127-37.

8. F. M. Dostojewski, *Was vermag der Mensch?— Ein Brevier*, selected and grouped, with an Introduction by Reinhard Lauth (Munich: R. Piper, 1949), p. 247.

9. *Ibid.*, p. 248.

10. Referring to this dual conception of man in Dostoevsky's work, Lossky considers it the main theme of Dostoevsky's writings: "All people retain, at least subconsciously, the connection with God and the Absolute Good and the ideal of their personal absolute perfection, the ideal of fullness of life. Man's destiny is dependent upon the extent of his love for these treasures. This is the main theme of Dostoevsky's fiction. If man prefers treasures other than God and his own perfection in God, inevitably his life will be belittled as a result of his isolation from others. This, in its turn, will lead him sooner or later to disappointment with all his aims and achievements in such an incomplete existence; to the entire dissatisfaction with his life, and to a greater or lesser degree of split personality."—N. Lossky, *Dostoevsky i ego khristianskoe miroponimanie* (New York: Chekhov, 1953), pp. 282-83.

2—The Technique of Dream-Logic

1. D. S. Mirsky, *A History of Russian Literature* (London: Routledge, 1949), p. 169.

2. E. M. de Vogüé, *Le Roman russe* (Paris: Plon, 1888), p. xxvi.

3. F. M. Dostojewski, "Notierte Gedanken, 1880" in *Was vermag der Mensch?—Ein Brevier* (Munich, 1949), p. 35.

4. *Dostoevsky—Pisma 1867-1871*, ed. and annotated by A. S. Dolinin (Moscow-Leningrad: Gos. Izdat., 1930), II, 169-70 (letter to N. N. Strakhov dated February 26, 1869).

5. J. C. Powys, *Dostoievsky* (London: John Lane, 1946), p. 36.

6. Ref. D. S. Merezhkovsky, *L. Tolstoy i Dostoevsky* (St. Petersburg: Mir iskusstva, 1901), pp. 280, 285, 296–97.

7. E. J. Simmons, *Dostoevski—the Making of a Novelist* (London: Oxford University Press, 1940), p. 56.

8. F. M. Dostoevsky, *Dnevnik pisatelya za 1877 god* (Paris: YMCA-Press, n.d.), p. 171.

9. D. Čyževskyj, "Zum Doppelgängerproblem bei Dostojevskij," in *Dostojevskij-Studien* (Reichenberg: Gebrüder Stlepel, 1931), pp. 20–21.

10. *PMLA*, LXXIII (March 1958), 101–9.

11. *Ibid.*, p. 103.

12. J. C. Powys, *Dostoievsky*, p. 36.

13. Ref. Dostoevsky's letters to his brother, Mikhail, dated February 1, 1846, and April 1, 1846, *Pisma 1832–1867* (Moscow-Leningrad, 1928), I, 86–87, 88–90.

14. *Dostoevsky: A Collection of Critical Essays*, ed. René Wellek (New York: Prentice-Hall, 1962), p. 26.

15. A. Bem, *Dostoevsky: Psikhoanaliticheskie etyudy* (Berlin: Speer & Schmidt, 1938), p. 69.

16. Dostoevsky seems to use dreams for developing thoughts for which, as he himself maintains in *The Diary of a Writer* and in some of his novels, ordinary language is inadequate. In *A Raw Youth* he interpolates an admission to this effect in Arkady Dolgoruky's speech: "There remains unsaid in an individual infinitely more than can be adequately put in word." Arkady is troubled not only by his inability to express satisfactorily his thoughts and more particularly his feelings, but also by his fear that, in the formulation, these ideas may lose something of their depth and value. "Our thoughts," he reflects, "even the least significant ones, are deeper so long as they remain within us. Once expressed, the same thoughts appear to us ridiculous and, as it were, dishonorable." (Cf. Tyutchev's famous line from "Silentium": "Mysl' izrechennaya est' lozh'"—"The thought expressed is a lie.") Similar statements and observations appear in many works of Dostoevsky. His characters often suffer because their experiences become distorted when put into words,

and consequently they are not taken seriously by their fellow men, as in the case of Ippolit or Prince Myshkin. As may be seen from *Netochka Nezvanova*, Dostoevsky attaches great importance to dreams, since he considers that they reveal not only the true nature of man, but also the predestined way of his spiritual growth. "There are moments," Dostoevsky says here, "in which all intellectual and spiritual strength is morbidly strained to a point where it suddenly flares up in a blazing flame of knowledge. At such an instant, the disturbed soul, tormented by presentiments of the future, has a prophetic dream. We then long to live; our entire being craves for it; and the heart becomes filled with a flaming, even if blind, hope, challenging, as it were, the unknown future with all its mystery, even if it should be full of violent storms and hurricanes, so long as it is also full of life." For Dostoevsky, the seeming absurdities of dreams, visions, presentiments, hallucinations, and other revelations of the irrational mind, hint at mysteries of cosmic proportions, which would be unveiled to man if he were but able to understand the symbolism of the message. Informed by his dreams, in which his restless unconscious announces its contents, the hero of Dostoevsky often perceives what is hidden within him. In this way he can see that the irrational aspects of his nature communicate directly with external forces which the rational mind cannot comprehend. In the interpretation of dreams Dostoevsky is similar to E. T. A. Hoffmann, who claimed that what is customarily called dream and fantasy is really the symbolical manifestation of the hidden thread running through man's life, and connecting it in all its parts. Maintaining that the human unconscious becomes manifest only in dreams and hallucinations, Hoffmann said, "in dream a strange voice informs us of things we did not know, or about which we were at least in doubt, regardless of the fact that the voice which seems to bring us strange knowledge really comes only from our own innermost being and speaks aloud in intelligible words." —E. T. A. Hoffmann, *Werke*, ed. W. Harich (Weimar, 1924), I, 181.

17. Some scholars have already treated this subject to a certain extent. See A. Bem, *Dostoevsky*, and R. Tymms, *Doubles in Literary Psychology* (Cambridge: Bowes and Bowes, 1949).

18. An exhaustive study of the influence of E. T. A. Hoffmann on the literary production of Dostoevsky is presented by C. E. Passage, in his book *Dostoevski the Adapter* (Chapel Hill: University of North Carolina Press, 1954). Passage admits the individuality of Dostoevsky's artistic method when he says, "He was the only one . . . who had the insight and the genius to dominate so large a model and to conceive so vast a plan of transformation" (p. 175). As Passage implies, in Dostoevsky's utilization of the borrowed elements, it is the transformation of the material in his hands and his own strong creative will which make his approach so strikingly original. See also V. Ya. Kirpotin, *F. M. Dostoevsky—Tvorchesky put' 1821–1859* (Moscow: GIKhL, 1960), p. 387.

Reference to the connection between Hoffmann and Dostoevsky in the treatment of schizophrenia is found in Tymms's study of the *Doppelgänger* problem. But, like Passage and Kirpotin, Tymms also points out the difference in their artistic method. "Dostoevsky was familiar with the romantic conception of the unconscious personality from his predilection for Hoffmann's works themselves," Tymms writes, "but he excludes the *diablerie* and supernaturalism that obscure Hoffmann's realism, nor does he dabble, as did his admired predecessor, in pseudo-philosophical and aesthetic speculation on the subject of the 'cosmic myth.' In spite, or because, of this austerity, his scientific realism is more horrifying than the feverish imaginings of the romantic tale of horror; for, as Merejkowsky remarks, . . . the light of science only makes the shadows more profound, and its introduction into literature creates a new *Schauerromantik* more terrifying than the old." (R. Tymms, *Doubles in Literary Psychology*, p. 98.)

19. C. G. Jung, *Gestaltungen des Unbewussten* (Zürich: Rascher, 1950).

20. Sigmund Freud, *Abriss der Psychoanalyse: Das*

Unbehagen in der Kultur (Frankfurt am Main, Hamburg: Fischer, 1950), p. 8.

3—Biographical Factors

1. J. A. T. Lloyd, *Fyodor Dostoevsky* (London: Eyre & Spottiswoods, 1946), p. 11.

2. H. Troyat, *Fireband—the Life of Dostoevsky* (New York: Roy Publishers, 1946), p. 37.

3. K. Mochulsky, *Dostoevsky* (Paris: YMCA-Press, 1947), p. 12.

4. *Biografiya, pisma i zametki iz zapisnoy knizhki F. M. Dostoevskogo* (St. Petersburg: Suvorin, 1883), p. 26.

5. A. G. Dostojewski, *Errinnerungen der Anna Grigorjewna Dostojewski* (Munich: R. Piper & Co., 1948), p. 71.

6. K. Nötzel, *Das Leben Dostojewskis* (Leipzig: H. Haessel, 1925), p. 7.

7. F. M. Dostoevsky, *Dnevnik pisatelya za 1876 god* (Paris, n.d.), p. 37.

8. D. V. Grigorovich, "Literaturnye vospominaniya," *Russkaya mysl'* (Moscow, 1892), December issue, pp. 13–17.

9. *Dostoevsky—Pisma 1832–1867* (Moscow-Leningrad, 1928), I, 52 (letter to Dostoevsky's father dated May 10, 1839).

10. *Ibid.*, I, 46 (letter to Dostoevsky's brother, Mikhail, dated August 9, 1838).

11. Ref. K. Nötzel, *Das Leben Dostojewskis*, p. 39.

12. A. G. Dostojewski, *Erinnerungen*, p. 89.

13. F. M. Dostoevsky, *Dnevnik pisatelya za 1877 god* (Paris, n.d.), p. 80.

14. F. M. Dostoevsky, *Sobranie sochineny* (Moscow: GIKhL, 1958), XI, 191.

15. Ref. Dostoevsky's letter to Mikhail from Omsk, dated February 22, 1854, *Dostoevsky—Pisma 1832–1867* (Moscow-Leningrad, 1928), I, 139.

16. F. M. Dostoevsky, *Sobranie sochineny* (1956), III, 701. F. Nietzsche, a later admirer of Dostoevsky,

referring to his observation about the convicts in Siberia, says: "Der Verbrecher-Typus ist . . . ein krank gemachter starker Mensch. . . . Dostoiewsky, der einziger Psychologe, anbei gesagt, von dem ich etwas zu lernen hatte: er gehört zu den schöhnsten Glückfällen meines Lebens, mehr selbst noch als die Entdeckung Stendahl's. Dieser *tiefe* Mensch, der zehn Mal Recht hatte, die oberflächlichen Deutschen gering zu schätzen, hat die sibirischen Zuchthäusler, in deren Mitte er lange lebte, lauter schwere Verbrecher, für die es keinen Rückweg zur Gesellschaft mehr gab, sehr anders empfunden, als er selbst erwartete —ungefähr als aus dem besten, härtesten und wertvollsten Holze geschnitzt, das auf russischer Erde überhaupt wächst." *Nietzsches Werke* (Leipzig: Alfred Kroner, n.d.), VIII, 183–84.

17. Ref. *From the Reminiscences of Baron Alexander Wrangel 1854–1865, Letters of Fyodor Mikhailovitch Dostoevsky to his Family and Friends,* tr. E. C. Mayne (London: Chatto & Windus, 1914), p. 298.

18. Besides the phenomenon of hypnosis, G. H. v. Schubert elaborates a theory of the dual self, with its "sidereal" and "adamitic" phases. Since the former, present in the human personality, participates in the life of the universe as a whole, it is more important than the "adamitic" phase. The latter, in contrast to the "sidereal," has relation to time and, as an external shell of the human individual, is often mistaken for man's basic character. Another important difference between the "sidereal" and "adamitic" selves is the former's usual silence. By hypnotic evocation, however, it becomes accessible and manifests itself in dreams, hallucinations, and premonitions.

19. S. Smith and A. Isotoff, "The Abnormal from Within: Dostoevsky," *Psychological Review* (Eugene: Oregon University Publications, 1935), XXII, No. 4, 347.

20. *Dostoevsky—Pisma 1832–1867,* I, 46 (letter to Mikhail dated August 9, 1838).

21. *Biografiya, pisma i zametki iz zapisnoy knizhki F. M. Dostoevskogo,* p. 214.

22. In a letter to E. F. Yunge, Dostoevsky confessed that throughout his life he was aware of his own duality. "Why do you wonder about your duality?" he wrote, "It is the commonest of human traits . . . that is, it is common to all who are not wholly commonplace. Nay, this trait is common to human nature in general, though it does not reveal itself so strongly in all as it does in you. It is on precisely these grounds that I regard you so akin to me, for your duality corresponds more exactly to my own. I have experienced my own duality throughout my whole life." Ref. Dostoevsky's letter to E. F. Yunge dated April 11, 1880, in *Dostoevsky—Pisma 1878–1881* (Moscow, 1959), IV, 136–37.

23. F. M. Dostoevsky, *Dnevnik pisatelya za 1877 god*, p. 30.

24. N. Zernov, *Three Russian Prophets: Khomiakov, Dostoevsky, Soloviev* (London: S. C. M. Press, 1944), p. 98.

25. F. M. Dostoevsky, *Dnevnik pisatelya za 1873 god* (Paris: YMCA-Press, n.d.), pp. 23–24.

26. F. M. Dostoevsky, *Dnevnik pisatelya za 1880 god* (Paris: YMCA-Press, n.d.), p. 7.

27. F. M. Dostoevsky, "Iz zapisnoy knizhki," *Novy put'* (St. Petersburg), February 1904, p. 1.

28. *Ibid.*, p. 7.

29. *Tvorchestvo Dostoevskogo 1821–1881–1921: Sbornik statey i materialov*, ed. L. P. Grossman (Odessa: Vseukrainskoe izdatelstvo, 1921), p. 15.

4—Symptoms of Spiritual Decay

1. Fedor Stepun, *Dostojewskij und Tolstoj—Christentum u. soziale Revolution* (Munich: C. Hauser, 1961), p. 29.

2. Alfred Adler, *Understanding Human Nature*, tr. W. B. Wolfe (London: G. Allen & Unwin, 1946), pp. 191–92.

3. *Ibid.*, pp. 193, 195.

4. F. M. Dostoevsky, *Dnevnik pisatelya za 1877 god* (Paris, n.d.), p. 400.

5. Alfred Adler, *Understanding Human Nature*, pp. 212–13.

6. *Dostoevsky—Pisma* 1832–1867 (Moscow-Leningrad, 1928), I, 46 (Dostoevsky's letter to Mikhail dated August 9, 1838).

7. Letter to A. N. Maykov dated January 12, 1868, and to S. A. Ivanova dated January 1, 1868, *Dostoevsky—Pisma 1867–1871* (Moscow-Leningrad, 1930), II, 61, 71.

8. *Iz arkhiva F. M. Dostoevskogo—Idiot—Neizdannye materialy—Tsentrarkhiv*, ed. by P. N. Sakulin and N. F. Belchikov (Moscow-Leningrad: GIKhL, 1931), pp. 126, 129, 133.

9. Martin Buber, *Bilder von Gut und Böse* (Köln: J. Hegner, 1953), p. 26.

10. *Dostoevsky—Pisma* 1832–1867, I, 50 (Dostoevsky's letter to Mikhail dated October 31, 1838).

11. F. M. Dostoevsky, *An Honest Thief and Other Stories* (London: Heinemann, 1950), p. 322.

12. *Dostoevsky—Pisma* 1832–1867, I, 50.

13. Ref. *Iz arkhiva F. M. Dostoevskogo—Prestuplenie i nakazanie—Neiznannye materialy—Tsentrarkhiv*, ed. and prepared for publication by I. I. Glivenko (Moscow-Leningrad: GIKhL, 1931), p. 83.

14. R. L. Jackson, *Dostoevsky's Underground Man in Russian Literature* (Gravenhage: Mouton & Co., 1958), p. 62.

15. F. M. Dostoevsky, *The Possessed* (London: Heinemann, 1951), p. 475.

16. *Dostoevsky—Pisma* 1878–1881 (Moscow, 1959), IV, 221 (letter dated December 19, 1880).

5—The Metaphysics of Evil

1. *Dostoevsky—Pisma 1832–1867* (Moscow-Leningrad, 1928), I, 46 (Dostoevsky's letter to Mikhail dated August 9, 1838).

2. *Ibid.*, I, 46.

3. Books II–IV, 445B, Chapter V (II.357A–367E).

4. *Dostoevsky—Pisma* 1832–1867, I, 50 (Dostoevsky's letter to Mikhail dated October 31, 1838).

5. F. M. Dostoevsky, *Dnevnik pisatelya za 1876 god* (Paris, n.d.), p. 476.

6. *Ibid.*, p. 46.

7. F. M. Dostojewski, *Was vermag der Mensch?— Ein Brevier* (Munich, 1949), pp. 247–48.

8. *F. M. Dostoevsky—Materialy i issledovaniya* (Leningrad, 1935), p. 281.

9. *Dostoevsky—Pisma 1878–1881* (Moscow, 1959), IV, 190 (Dostoevsky's letter to N. A. Lyubimov dated August 10, 1880).

10. *Dostoevsky: A Collection of Critical Essays* (New York, 1962), p. 92.

6—The Spiritual Goal

1. F. M. Dostoevsky, *Dnevnik pisatelya za 1876 god* (Paris, n.d.), p. 476.

2. *Ibid.*, p. 474.

3. *Ibid.*, pp. 473–74.

4. *Ibid.*, p. 46.

5. *O Dostoevskom—Sbornik statey*, ed. A. L. Bem (Prague, 1929), I, 162.

6. Fedor Stepun, *Dostojewskij und Tolstoj—Christentum u. soziale Revolution* (Munich, 1961), p. 29.

7. *Dostoevsky—Pisma 1867–1871* (Moscow-Leningrad, 1930), II, 25 (Dostoevsky's letter to A. N. Maykov dated August 28, 1867).

8. W. Hubben, *Four Prophets of Our Destiny* (New York: Macmillan, 1952), p. 68.

9. L. A. Zander, *Dostoevsky*, tr. N. Duddington (London: S. C. M. Press, 1948), p. 44.

10. F. M. Dostoevsky, *Dnevnik pisatelya za 1876 god*, p. 61. It must be noted that with his idealization of the Russian common people and their way of life, Dostoevsky shared the fundamental conviction of the *narodniki* (or "populists") that the salvation of Russia lay in the Russian peasantry. Dostoevsky's cult of the Russian peasant, however, had a moral and philosophic coloring, and had, therefore, very little in common with a radical

political movement of the 1870's, 1880's, and 1890's. *Narodniki* were those members of the Russian intelligentsia who considered a revolution desirable and regarded the peasantry as the chief means of accomplishing this revolution. They believed that the basis for agrarian socialism existed in the traditional peasant institutions such as the *mir* with its communal land tenure. Dostoevsky's conviction that the secret of universal harmony is grasped by the heart and by religious faith, was, of course, a far cry from the revolutionary ardor of the "populists" to establish equality and justice by force.

11. F. M. Dostoevsky, "Iz zapisnoy knizhki," *Novy put'* (St. Petersburg), February 1904, p. 6.

12. F. M. Dostoevsky, *Dnevnik pisatelya za 1880 god* (Paris, n.d.), p. 553.

13. *Ibid.*, p. 553.

14. *Dostoevsky—Pisma 1878–1881* (Moscow, 1959), IV, 5 (Dostoevsky's letter to N. L. Ozmidov dated February, 1878).

15. F. M. Dostoevsky, *Dnevnik pisatelya za 1880 god*, p. 552.

16. *F. M. Dostoevsky—Materialy i issledovaniya* (Leningrad, 1935), p. 154.

17. *Iz arkhiva F. M. Dostoevskogo—Prestuplenie i nakazanie—Neizdannye materialy—Tsentrarkhiv* (Moscow-Leningrad, 1931), p. 167.

18. *Ibid.*, p. 167.

19. *Dostoevsky—Pisma 1867–1871*, II, 284 (Dostoevsky's letter to S. A. Ivanova dated August 17, 1870).

20. F. M. Dostoevsky, *Dnevnik pisatelya za 1880 god*, p. 501.

21. F. M. Dostoevsky, *Dnevnik pisatelya za 1877 god* (Paris, n.d.), p. 284.

22. F. M. Dostojewski, *Was vermag der Mensch?— Ein Brevier* (Munich, 1949), pp. 123–24.

23. *Ibid.*, pp. 97–98.

24. *Ibid.*, p. 109.

25. F. M. Dostoevsky, *An Honest Thief and Other Stories* (London: Heinemann, 1950), p. 231.

26. F. M. Dostojewski, *Was vermag der Mensch?—Ein Brevier*, p. 118.

7—Psychology of Goodness

1. N. Gorodetzky, *The Humiliated Christ in Modern Russian Thought* (New York: Macmillan, 1938), p. 65.

2. *F. M. Dostoevsky—Materialy is issledovaniya* (Leningrad, 1935), p. 147. *See also The Brothers Karamazov*, Chapter "The Russian Monk": "Life is paradise, and we are all in paradise, but we do not wish to see it. If we wished, we would have Heaven on earth the next day." "Heaven lies hidden within all of us. Here it lies hidden in me now, and if I will it, it will be revealed to me tomorrow and for all time."

3. Cf. John 1:29: "The next day John seeth Jesus coming unto him, and saith, 'Behold the Lamb of God, which taketh away the sin of the world.'"

4. Ref. *Iz arkhiva F. M. Dostoevskogo—Idiot—Neizdannye materialy—Tsentrarkhiv* (Moscow-Leningrad, 1931), pp. 126, 129, 133.

5. *Dostoevsky—Pisma 1867–1871* (Moscow-Leningrad, 1930), II, 148 (Dostoevsky's letter to A. N. Maykov dated December 11, 1868).

6. *Ibid.*, II, 138 (Dostoevsky's letter to S. A. Ivanova dated October 26, 1868).

7. *Ibid.*, II, 111 (Dostoevsky's letter to S. A. Ivanova dated April 10, 1868).

8. E. J. Simmons, *Dostoevski: the Making of a Novelist* (London, 1940), pp. 230–31.

9. Murray Krieger, "Dostoevsky's *Idiot*: The Curse of Saintliness," *Dostoevsky: A Collection of Critical Essays* (New York, 1962), pp. 48, 51.

10. F. M. Dostoevsky, *A Raw Youth* (London: Heinemann, 1950), p. 6.

11. F. M. Dostoevsky, *Crime and Punishment*, tr. D. Magashack (Harmondsworth: Penguin Books, 1951), p. 40.

12. Matthew 10:34–36.

13. F. M. Dostojewski, *Was vermag der Mensch?—Ein Brevier* (Munich, 1949), pp. 125–26.

8—Dostoevsky's Ultimate Answer

1. *Dostoevsky—Pisma* 1832–1867 (Moscow-Leningrad, 1928), I, 129 (Dostoevsky's letter to Mikhail dated December 22, 1849).

2. *F. M. Dostoevsky—Materialy i issledovaniya* (Leningrad, 1935), p. 340.

3. *Ibid.*, p. 263.

4. R. Guardini, *Religiose Gestalten in Dostojewskijs Werk* (Munich: Hochland-Verlag, 1951), pp. 217–18.

5. "Iz zapisnoy knizhki F. M. Dostoevskogo," as quoted by A. S. Dolinin in *F. M. Dostoevsky—Materialy i issledovaniya,* p. 80.

9—Conclusion

1. Ref. M. M. Bakhtin, *Problemy tvorchestva Dostoevskogo* (Leningrad: Priboy, 1929). Bakhtin claimed that Dostoevsky had created the new type of novel, the "polyphonic," or many-voiced, novel. For a more extended treatment of Bakhtin's thesis, see V. Seduro's *Dostoyevski in Russian Literary Criticism 1846–1956* (New York: Columbia University Press, 1957), pp. 202–32.

2. N. Berdjajew, *Die Weltanschauung Dostojewskijs,* tr. W. E. Groeger (Munich: Becksche Verlagsbuchhandlung, 1925), p. 44.

3. *Dostoevsky—Pisma* 1832–1867 (Moscow-Leningrad, 1928), I, 86 (Dostoevsky's letter to Mikhail dated February 1, 1846).

4. V. V. Zenkovsky, "Dostoevsky's Religious and Philosophical Views," *Dostoevsky: A Collection of Critical Essays* (New York, 1962), p. 144.

INDEX